WORDS OF EXPRESSION

For you her readers from her heart as given to her by Christ Jesus Our Lord and Savior. May she always write with an anointed hand and be blessed forever.

—**Doretha C. Robinson**
Mother of Prophetess Elizabeth Perkins

Pastor Elizabeth Perkins is one of the most dynamic preachers of this century. Based on her experiences, both personal and spiritual, she has written a truthful book. The value of this book cannot be overemphasized besides being enlightened and convicting. It is inspiring and motivational. This is a must read! *The Fight Of My Life*!

—**Apostle Ketrenea Owens**
Pastor of Destiny Of Faith International
Spring, Texas

Little did I know I was in the presence of greatness when Sr. Pastor Elizabeth Perkins walked into the beauty salon promoting her book – *Excess Baggage*. Our meeting was divinely ordained by God to get her to our church – The Living Word Faith Center. We did not know the chance meeting would be the backdrop to the real fight of her life and I would watch God perform His healing miracle. You too will experience healing and deliverance while reading this book because you are in the Fight Of Your Life!

—**Pastor Janet Bradford**
Missouri City, Texas

Author, Pastor and Intercessor, Elizabeth Perkins has a unique skill to motivate women from all walks of life. The prophetic utterance of God and her contrite heart allows her to flow in such a profound, yet practical manner that readers are shaped and put at ease by her words. After reading her second book, Woman Behind The Mask, I waited with anticipation for her next bestseller and here it is, The Fight Of My Life!

Evangelist Tammina Ford
Houston, Texas

I have known Pastor Elizabeth Perkins for several years and her love for God and her passion for Ministry has been a blessing to me. Along with her life experiences, God has given her wisdom and knowledge to bring hope, healing and deliverance to women of all ages. She is anointed and gifted not only to write, but also to stand and minister the Word of God to His people. She is truly an asset to the Body of Christ.

Pastor C.I. Carter
Sr. Pastor of Williams Temple
Church Of God In Christ
Houston, Texas

Prophetess Elizabeth Perkins has a unique ministry that has touched the lives of women to come out from behind their mask. She moves in power, healing and deliverance. As God continues to unfold and unveil her Prophetic mantle, she is only at the tip of the iceberg.

Apostle, Dr. Rhonda Travitt
Sr. Pastor & Founder of
Restoring The Years Global Ministries
Marietta, Georgia

The Fight Of My Life

The Fight Of My Life

Is There Anything Too Hard For The Lord?

ELIZABETH PERKINS

FOREWORD BY APOSTLE JOHN LOUIS HICKMAN

The Fight Of My Life

Copyright © 2019 by Elizabeth Perkins

First Printing, December 2019
First Edition, December 2019

Elizabeth Perkins Ministries
PowerInTheWordFellowship.org
Office: 832-250-1860

Unless otherwise indicated, all scripture quotations are taken from The King James Version, The New International Version, The Message Bible and The Living Bible. Used by permission.

Any definitions used are taken from the Webster's Unabridged Dictionary, Second Edition. Used by permission.

All rights reserved under International Copyright Law. No part of this publication may be reproduced, stored in a retrieval system or transmitted in any form or by any means for example, electronic, photocopy, recording, used for ministerial training, ministerial teaching or educational training without the prior written permission of the author or publisher.

Printed In The United States of America

ISBN: 978-0-578-85012-2

TO MY LORD

As I walked through the valley of the shadow of death and the Fight Of My Life, you never left me. Therefore, with all of my heart and soul, I dedicate this story to you and only you Lord – full of truth, trust, turns, trials, tribulations and triumph.

Lord, I thank you for giving me the will to fight during a time when I wanted to give up on my life and destiny. Instead of allowing sickness and death to rob me of your divine plan from the foundation of the world, you released your healing virtue, your grace and mercy and gave me a miracle only you could give.

Thank you for being Savior, Redeemer and Healer. There is no other God besides you. I give you all the praise and all the glory not only because you healed me – but because you heard my cry. For this reason, may my life give you glory. May my story and testimony empower others to see there is nothing too hard for the Lord. Amen.

DEDICATION

To My Pastor, *The Chief Apostle, Dr. John Louis Hickman, Sr. Pastor of The Living Word Faith Center in Missouri City, Texas.* Thank you for every apostolic word, prophetic prayer and faith you released in my life that caused my healing to be manifested from the spiritual to the natural. While I was coming through what seemed like the storm of my life and the trial of my soul, you told me 'I would live and not die.'

While I was in the delivery room believing God for my healing and experiencing *the fight of my life*, you prayed for me. Therefore, I salute you with full honors in the Kingdom of the Lord. May the God of heaven and earth continue to use you to transform what most people call 'ordinary' lives to 'extraordinary' and use the healing and deliverance anointing that rest on your life to deliver souls and set the captive free for His Kingdom and for His Glory.

DEDICATION FOR MOMMA

To *Ms. Doretha Robinson* ("My Momma") of Orange, Texas who I call "Momma" but, I also call her my "Friend." On the night when the spirit of death was upon me, you prayed for me. It was then I entered – *the fight of my life*. After you released words of prayer over me and lay your body across mine, the spirit of death which hovered over me, left me and departed the room.

Through some of my darkest days and moments which were full of clouds and sounds of rain and thunder, you were there for me while I was crawling my way out of the valley. As my life has been under construction for a number of years and my wings have now been repaired in the chambers of the Almighty God, I thank you for allowing me to rest under your wings until I regained my strength so I could fly again.

With love and honor towards you "Momma", may I carry the seed of greatness the Lord Jesus Christ gave me and fulfill my destiny. Thank you for all the days you watered that seed, told me to keep moving and never look back no matter what. You have always been my inspiration and you still are. In Jesus Mighty Name. Amen.

SPECIAL DEDICATION

To *Renee Petis*, P. A. ("Doctor Petis") of Houston, Texas who walked with me during the fight of my life. When I was facing fear and doubt, you told me with compassion and love – God was in control and everything was going to be alright. Thank you for your words of encouragement and your faith in Jesus Christ Our Lord and Savior.

May the Lord who sits high and looks down low always bless you and use you as an instrument of encouragement. You are awesome! You are the most priceless P. A. on this side of heaven! In Jesus Mighty Name. Amen.

SPECIAL DEDICATION

Little did I know, I would meet the woman and the midwife Pastor Janet Bradford who the Lord used to escort me to the next place where I would be healed.

I did not meet her by accident, but on purpose from the Lord. She was the anchor God used to pray for me and minister to my soul when I was fighting for my life.

I will be forever grateful for the power that she carries as an intercessor in the Kingdom of God.

TABLE OF CONTENTS

Preface………..….………………………………………….....xix

Foreword…………......……………………………………......xxiii

Introduction………....……....……………………………….....1

SECTION 1

THE FIRST FIGHT — *FIGHTING FOR MY LIFE*

CHAPTER 1
This Is Your Final Warning…………………...………………..9

CHAPTER 2
Don't Play With Your Purpose……....…………………....……19

CHAPTER 3
Don't Go Back In The Room………………………...…………29

CHAPTER 4
Something About Momma…......……………..……………....41

CHAPTER 5
Something Is Wrong…………………………………………49

CHAPTER 6
My Doctor Called…………………………………………..…59

CHAPTER 7
I Remember That Day…..69

CHAPTER 8

When The Righteous Cry..81

SECTION 2

THE SECOND FIGHT — *FIGHTING FOR MY MIND*

CHAPTER 9

Whose Report Will You Believe?..95

CHAPTER 10

Is There Anything Too Hard For The Lord?............................ 105

CHAPTER 11

The Waiting Room...115

CHAPTER 12

The Battle In My Mind..125

CHAPTER 13

The Battle In My Body..135

SECTION 3

THE THIRD FIGHT — *FIGHTING FOR MY PURPOSE*

CHAPTER 14

Your Faith Must Stand Trial...151

CHAPTER 15

The Delivery Room... 161

CHAPTER 16

While You Are Waiting 171

CHAPTER 17

Somebody Needs Prayer..181

CHAPTER 18

Long Days And Long Nights..191

SECTION 4

THE FOURTH FIGHT—*FIGHTING FOR MY HEALING*

CHAPTER 19

You Will Live And Not Die...205

CHAPTER 20

I Know It Was the Blood.. 215

CHAPTER 21

Sunday Morning Power Prayer..225

CHAPTER 22

When Praises Go Up...235

CHAPTER 23

Do You Believe In Miracles?..245

CHAPTER 24

The Fight Of My Life.. 255

PREFACE

I remembered the shattering news I received in **June 2013**. I experienced the nightmare of my life. In my mind, I received a death sentence. I had a bad report from my doctor. At that moment, my heart dropped and my tears overflowed and rolled down my face.

I was devastated. It was too much for me to handle. It was too much for me to comprehend. Almost immediately, I thought my life would be shortened and interrupted in ways I never imagined because of this condition. It was not a mistake. It was the truth. The Word of God even says in I John 1:18, *"If we say we have no sin, we deceive ourselves, and the truth is not in us."* (KJV)

I had HIV. I knew what it felt like. Moreover, I realized what others endured, including the private shame and public ridicule which came along with it. I was now one of them. I could feel their pain. I could see their tears. I could hear their cry.

One of the most difficult things I experienced was hearing those words from the doctor – *"You tested positive for HIV!"* From that hour, I was never the same again. For a brief moment, there was complete silence in the room. Soon thereafter, all I did was cried. My tears kept falling as if there was no end. I felt paralyzed. I felt numb. I felt devastated. I felt totally contaminated.

As I sat back and thought about the words and sentences in this story of truth, trials, test, tribulations and testimony, I had to exhale because this book was like no other. I reflected where I was then and where I am now. I am so incredibly grateful to be able to tell my story of how the Lord healed me. In Jeremiah

17:14, *the scriptures illustrates, "Heal me, O Lord, and I shall be healed; save me, and I shall be saved: for thou art my praise."* (KJV)

For this reason alone, I must tell it all. I wanted to tell this story from beginning to the end. This was the very thing I promised the Lord. I made a vow to Him to share this truth and testimony with the world. According to Psalm 24:1, the Bible states, *"The earth is the Lord's, and the fullness thereof; the world, and they that dwell therein."*(KJV)

This story belonged to the Lord and all of His glory. In the Word of God it displays these words, *"I am the Lord: that is my name: and my glory will I not give to another, neither my praise to graven images."* Isaiah 42:8 (KJV) Therefore, it had to be told.

As such, this composition caused me to write about various areas in my life which would be personal, private and painful to say the least. Yet, I recognized this book had to be written no matter what it would cost me. Regardless if I was judged, criticized or crucified, the Lord deserved the honor.

The world needed to hear and know about the grace, mercy and unconditional love of God and His healing anointing. That is why the Bible says, *"Let us therefore come boldly unto the throne of grace that we may obtain mercy, and find grace to help in time of need."* Hebrews 4:16. (KJV) The Lord brought me out of what seemed like a grave condition.

In my heart, I slowly found the courage to put my hands into the hands of the Lord to unravel this truth. The Lord deserved every speckle of glory. He deserved all of the praise. Because of the miracle and supernatural healing that occurred, I could not deny the Lord what rightfully belonged to Him. I did not imagine all I would go through as the chapters of my life unfolded. In the end, I discovered I was headed on another journey of learning many hard lessons in life. Unfortunately, there are certain lessons you learn which can only be understood afterwards, even if there is suffering, embarrassment, hurt and pain involved in the process of learning. However, if you allow those lessons to work for your good, they bring you to levels of *growth, maturity, humility and compassion* for others which would have never arrived without you understanding the value of each of those lessons.

Nevertheless, this book had to come forth. This narrative had to be told since the outcome was not due to me, but because the Lord deserved to be glorified for what He had done in my earthen vessel.

—The Fight Of My Life
Prophetess Elizabeth Perkins, M.A.
Founder Of Power In The Word Fellowship

FOREWORD

This book represents the healing power and virtue the Lord still provides. Moreover, it decrees and declares in the supernatural what happens when you believe. According to the Word of God, the woman with the issue of blood bled for 12 long years. *She bled for 4,380 days continuously until she said, "If I may but touch the hem of his garment, I shall be healed."* Mark 5:25(KJV) Because of her faith, this woman stepped into a dimension and received her healing. From that moment, she was healed.

In 2013, Prophetess and Pastor Elizabeth Perkins was diagnosed with HIV. After her long fight through prayer, deliverance and faith, she was healed by the Lord in 2014. She won the fight. Nevertheless, the Lord won the battle and gave her the victory. Her testimony is like no other. It is real. It is true. She won the fight of her life.

—**Apostle, Dr. John Louis Hickman**
Founder and Senior Pastor,
The Living Word Faith Center of International Churches
Missouri City, Texas

A Hard Truth Is Better Than A Long Lie

From The Author –

The Fight Of My Life
Prophetess Elizabeth Perkins, M.A.

INTRODUCTION

Have you ever been in a fight? Have you ever been in a fight for your life? What about the kind of fight where you received a bad report from the doctor and it stated you had a disease, a condition or an illness and maybe you were on the verge of dying and leaving your place on earth before your set time? What was the first thing that crossed your mind? Perhaps, you asked yourself some questions such as, *"Am I about to die?" "Did this come down my family blood line?" "How did I get this disease?"* or *"How did this condition get to me?"* Who was the first person you thought about? Did you think about your Father or your Mother? Did you wonder about your family or those who love you and you would leave them behind a little too soon? What was your immediate reaction?

What was going on inside the chambers of your heart when you heard the doctor call your name from the report to verify it was you? How did you respond? What was the condition of your mind? How did you feel emotionally?

How did you react when it was revealed to you? What was the name of your fight? Did you begin to cry, pray, or go into an immediate state of shock? Were you able to see the thing you were fighting against? Did you know how long your fight would last?

I definitely did not know how long my fight would last because the name of my fight was HIV. *HIV is defined as Human Immunodeficiency Virus.* That was my condition. That is why I wrote this book. That is why I chose to tell my story. I thought I was going to die.

I believe on some days, I wanted to die, although I asked the Lord to heal me. I was scared, frightened and terrified all at the same time. Quite obviously, I did not know which way things were going to go or how this situation was going to end. I recognized for sure I was in the fight of my life. This fight was real. This fight was serious.

Even though I could not see it with my natural eyes, the HIV was in my bloodstream. It was there. I felt the pain almost every day. I felt the attack on my immune system and my body. My fight seemed forever. It felt like an eternity. It felt like hell was unleashed against me.

While I was waiting and believing for the Lord to heal me, I made Him a definite promise. As I cried aloud and poured out every tear in my soul to my Father, I made Him a vow. I told Him as I lay prostrate before Him on my floor every morning, every day and every night, I would release my testimony to the world if He healed me. I was holding on to every prophetic word of healing, prayer, and faith waiting on the Lord to render His verdict in His heavenly courtroom.

It was almost a year later the miracle I stood on in prayer and reached for in the spiritual realm came true. It manifested itself from the natural to the supernatural. The contamination in my blood from HIV was completely removed. The Lord brought it to past. The Lord healed me from HIV. It was not the doctors. It was not the medicine. It was the Lord.

After the Lord healed me, I did not have a right to keep this testimony to myself. It was too large for me to carry. It contained too much of the glory of God to keep it to myself. It was too much of a testimony for me not to share with others that the Lord is still a healer for those from all walks of life – no matter what their past contained.

The Lord carried me through every dark day, every long night and the valley where it seemed I resided for most of those months. He set me free from a blood disease which there is still no cure. He set me free from a disease where I took no medicine. He healed me supernaturally.

I was now included in the miracles Jesus performed in an earthen vessel. I felt like I touched Him just like the woman who had the issue in her blood. *When she heard of Jesus, she came in behind the crowd and touched his garment.* Mark 5:27 (KJV)

His healing virtue and anointing interrupted the disease in my blood stream and body. *And Jesus, immediately knowing in himself that virtue had gone out of him, turned him about in the press, and said, "Who touched my clothes?"* Mark 5:30 (KJV) It was a real miracle which could not be denied. Moreover, I recognized it was not just for me. This miracle was for others too. Others could be healed and set free too.

Without a doubt, the grace and mercy and love of God was demonstrated. He healed me by His Word and by the power of faith. I know God is a healer. His name is Jehovah Nissi, Our Healer. For that reason, He is the only true God.

Elizabeth Perkins

"I, even I, am the LORD; and beside me there is no Savior," according to Isaiah 43:11.(NIV) He is the one who deserves all the glory. The Lord not only healed me, but He was with me during...

The Fight Of My Life

*When I say unto the wicked
Thou shalt surely die
And thou givest him not warning
Nor speakest to warn
The wicked from his wicked way
To save his life
The same wicked man shall die
In his iniquity; but the blood
Will I require at thy hand.*

—Ezekiel 3:17, 18 (KJV)

Section 1

The First Fight: Fighting For My Life

CHAPTER 1

This Is Your Final Warning

LESSON

1

A warning is something sent by The Lord to get your immediate attention and to let you know there is a serious matter which involves your life. However, it is also a specific word or message given by God to let you know the enemy is preparing to set up a strategic strategy to destroy your name, kill your purpose and eliminate your destiny from the face of the earth. As a result, when you are called by God, He sends His love through His warnings which always come before destruction is hurled your way by the hand and plan of the enemy.

Wherefore let him that thinketh he standeth take heed lest he fall. There hath no temptation taken you but such as is common to man.
I Corinthians 10:12-13 (KJV)

So, if you think you are standing firm, be careful that you don't fall! No temptation has seized you except what is common to man.
I Corinthians 10:12-13 (NIV)

Our positions in the story are parallel – they at the beginning, we at the end – and we are just as capable of messing it up as they were. Don't be so naive and self-confident.
I Corinthians 10:12-13 (MSB)

So be careful. If you are thinking, "Oh, I would never behave like that" – let this be a warning to you. For you too may fall into sin."
I Corinthians 10:12-13 (TLB)

Why didn't I walk away after I received a warning from the Lord? Why didn't I take His words seriously? If I would've listened and not walked in my fleshly desires, I wouldn't have had to fight for my life. To be totally honest, a hard truth is better than a long lie.

One summer day, I was out promoting and selling my first book, *Excess Baggage, How Much Are You Carrying?*, in a barber and beauty shop I often visited in Humble, Texas. However, this day was a little different. When I walked in the shop, I decided to pass my book out to several people at once in order to possibly make more sells that day because I had a set goal in mind I wanted to achieve. Also, I needed to pay some bills that week. So, my book sells were vital Saturday.

Nonetheless, when I approached one particular gentleman, he asked me, *"Is this your book?"* I responded, *"Yes, of course."* He said, *"Is this you on the back?"* I told him, *"Yes, that is me."* He questioned me again, *"Are you the author of the book?"* I said, *"Yes."*

He appeared to be somewhat different and stared directly at me. He gawked at the book several times. Then, he gazed at me once more, but with seriousness and intensity as if he wanted to say something to me or needed to release a word of importance.

I was hoping he wanted to purchase a book since I had a few financial obligations on my plate. I was already out for a number of hours selling my book and the day was getting late. I was hoping he would purchase a book or two. So, as usual, I was waiting patiently.

All of a sudden, he glanced at me with sharp eyes and fatal intentions and he said, *"You know that guy you are seeing? He is bad news!"* When he released those words, I stood there for a minute or two. I was immediately convicted because I knew those words came straight from the Lord. According to the Word in Amos 3:7, *"For the Lord does nothing without revealing His secret to his servants the prophets."* (KJV) Those words hit my heart and my soul like a large boulder which tumbled down from a high mountain or a cliff heading directly towards me.

Initially, I did not know what to say. I could not deny the words I heard. I knew they were from the Lord. They were all true. The Bible says in Ezekiel 33:6-7, *"But if the watchman sees the sword coming and does not blow the trumpet, so that the people are not warned, and the sword comes and takes away any one of them, that person is taken away in his iniquity, but his blood I will require at the watchman's hand. "So you, son of man, I have made a watchman for the house of Israel. Whenever you hear a word from my mouth, you shall give them warning from me."* (KJV)

I realized the Lord sent him to deliver those words specifically to me. They seemed hard, but they were full of truth. *To be quite honest, a hard truth is better than a long lie!* On that day, the truth from heaven came down to visit me and arrest me from the road of calamity and the death of destruction. As it is written in Proverbs 16:18, *"Pride goes before destruction, and a haughty spirit before stumbling."* (KJV)

Although my walk with the Lord included some low places and dark valleys, I always repented to the Lord and followed Him wholeheartedly with seriousness and total commitment. Nevertheless, I found myself slowly drifting away from my place of prayer and consecration. I was walking in the lust of the eyes, the lust of the flesh and the pride of life. The Word of God states," *Let no man say when he is tempted, I am tempted of God: or God cannot be tempted with evil, neither be tempted he any man: But every man is tempted, when he is drawn away of his own lust and enticed.* James 1:14 (KJV)

I desired a relationship. A relationship with a genuine covenant. Not one with temporary convenience. With that being said, he said all the things I wanted to hear. He spoke all of the right words. They seemed so real. However, there was no real evidence to match his words. That is why the Word of God reads in I John 4:1, *"Beloved, do not believe every spirit, but test the spirits to see whether they are from God, for many false prophets have gone out into the world."* (KJV)

The first place where the enemy set up his plan of destruction, deceit and deception was in my mind and in my heart. *The word deception is defined as to make a person believe what is not true. Another meaning for this word is to be underhanded, to trap, ensnare or be untruthful.* (Webster's Dictionary)Truthfully, my heart, my mind and my desires were in the wrong place and in the wrong season.

Nonetheless, I still participated in the deception. I hated to face this reality. *I said some words I should not have stated. I took the bait from the enemy and I ate the bait as well. The enemy was working full time to overthrow my destiny.* That is why the Word of God states, *"The thief cometh not, but for to steal and to kill and to destroy; I am come that they might have life, and that they might have it more abundantly."* John 10:10 (KJV)

I realized the words spoke and some of them which were released went straight to my heart. According to Hebrews 4:12, it reads like this, *"For word of God is quick, and powerful, and sharper than any two edged sword, piercing even to the dividing asunder of soul and spirit, and of the joints and marrow, and is a discerner of the thoughts and intents of the heart."* (KVJ) As a result of me opening my heart, walking in sin, desiring to believe, not heeding to the Word and the warning from the Lord, my life was about to change not for the better – but for the worse.

CHAPTER 2
Don't Play With Your Purpose

LESSON

2

When you play with your purpose, you will either end up contaminating your assignment, missing your season and most of all, missing the destiny God had for your life. Yet, instead of you fulfilling your original purpose, you will become a cheap copy of something else or somebody else. In the end, your true purpose will evaporate because you decided to play with it instead of pursuing it – according to the perfect will of God.

The Lord of hosts hath sworn, saying, Surely as I have thought, so shall it come to pass; and as I have purposed, so shall it stand.
Isaiah 14:24 (KJV)

The Lord Almighty has sworn, Surely, as I have planned, so it will be, and as I have purposed, so it will stand.
Isaiah 14:24 (NIV)

God of the Angel Armies speaks: "Exactly as I planned, it will happen. Following my blueprints, it will take shape.
Isaiah 14:24 (MSB)

He has taken an oath to do it! For this is his purpose and plan.
Isaiah 14:24 (TLB)

This one thing is real and definite in life. When you play with the purpose God gave you, you lessen your worth and you devalue your purpose.

A fter I received a warning from the Lord, I attempted to resettle myself back into the Word and the things of the Lord. From time to time, it was hard to close the door I opened and remove myself from the relationship I started because I was still struggling with depression, loneliness, the desire to be loved and the –courage to be healed from the pains of my past. *In other words, if you do not have the courage to be healed from the pains of your pasts and the contamination of your past sins, then most likely, you will have the courage to live contaminated with the pains of your past and your current sins.* As it is written,in Matthew 11: 28-29, the Lord says, *"Come to me, all who labor and are heavy laden, and I will give you rest. Take my yoke upon you, and learn from me, for I am gentle and lowly in heart, and you will find rest for your souls."* (KJV) As much as I tried to rest on some days, my rest did not come easy, particularly in my heart and soul.

I was struggling with many things and especially my – quiet sins. *The definition of a quiet sin is the ability to sin by yourself or within your own private surroundings yet, function as if what you are doing is not sin at all.* Hence,I allowed myself to be distracted with the things of the flesh. According to Galatians 5:17, *"For the flesh lusteth against the*

Spirit, and the Spirit against the flesh: and these are contrary the one to the other: so that ye cannot do the things that ye would." (KJV)

Walking in the flesh included being involved in a relationship which I received a warning from the Lord as well as areas in my life which were not beneficial for my spiritual growth and everyday life. In the book of James 4:7, the Bible says, *"Submit yourselves therefore to God. Resist the devil and he will flee from you."* (KJV) However, you cannot resist the devil and expect him to flee from you when you are keeping him as a companion or weekly company.

Therefore, as much as I loved the Lord, I was not pleasing Him the way I use too. My desire for pleasing Him was confiscated and watered down. I slowly let down my spiritual guards. I gradually stopped putting on the whole Armor of God. It clearly states in Ephesians Chapter 6: 11-12, *"Put on the whole armour of God, that ye may be able to stand against the wiles of the devil. For we wrestle not against flesh and blood, but against principalities, against powers, against the rulers of the darkness of this world, against spiritual wickedness in high places.* (KJV)The enemy had an open invitation to frustrate and destroy my purpose because I refused to put on my spiritual armor, close the door to sin and put a spiritual lock on my commitment to the Lord.

I realized of course, the purpose the Lord gave me before the foundations of the world was calling me and the healing I craved. However, I was not ready for the process of what it would take to be healed. I was not ready to yield myself to His perfect will. In other words, I desired to do more fleshly things instead of focusing on my assignment and yielding myself to my destiny. In Matthew 7:21, the Bible illustrates,

"Not every one that saith unto me, Lord, Lord, shall enter into the Kingdom of heaven; but he that doeth the will of my Father which is in heaven." (KJV)

I was focusing on other affections instead of my purpose. Since I chose not to focus, I lived my life for a season chasing temporary things I thought I lost or I thought I missed. Hence, you cannot move forward in life or in the Lord, if you are still looking backwards. Besides, when you keep looking backwards, the things or the people you left behind, particularly the bad ones which caused you to sin – will be looking for you too!

Have you ever lived during a season in your life where you lived more in your past than focusing on the future? Yet, instead of you reaching for the things that were in front of you, you continued to reach backwards chasing and looking for things that you thought you lost? Quite frankly, that is a perfect recipe for a spiritual disaster or train wreck waiting to happen. At that time in my life, I refused to move forward. As a result, I lost valuable time and moreover, specific doors the Lord wanted to open.

Therefore, I played with a valuable season the Lord prepared for me. Sadly, when refuse to go forward in your life, you will end up going backwards! When you decide to go backwards, it may include being in an unhealthy relationship, ungodly relationships, destructive behaviors and fleshly soul ties. The truth is, you may not think you are playing with your purpose. However, when you refuse to obey God with the plans He has established for your life, then rest assure, you are now mishandling and wasting the purpose God created for you.

In the end, you will pay for playing with your purpose. **Purpose is defined as the reason for which something is** *created or exist.* (Webster's Dictionary) ***Playing is defined as to engage in an activity for enjoyment and recreation rather than the serious reason intended.*** (Webster's Dictionary) When you accept the full responsibility and recognize you played with your purpose and the enemy, you will realize you played with the season God planned to launch your ministry and perhaps elevate you in His Kingdom. Let me say this! Your purpose is a terrible thing to waste! Don't play with your purpose!

In Ecclesiastes 3:9, it states this, *"To everything there is a season, and a time to every purpose under the heaven."* So, when you play with your purpose, you will miss your set season. As a result, you will have to wait for your next season to come around regardless of how long it may take. ***Since you made God wait on you – you will now have to wait on God! Remember, God says in His word, "I change not!"***Malachi 3:6 (KJV)

The conclusion of the matter is this: when you play with your purpose, the enemy will play with you! He will invite you into a spiral of delays, dark roads, denial and destruction. Slowly, but surely, envy, competition and jealousy will quietly set in your heart. ***The definition of jealousy is to have resentment, bitterness or to be unhappy against a person enjoying success, life and peace.*** Hence, you may not lose your total purpose, but you will definitely feel ashamed, embarrassed and even angry because you missed the season God had for you. Now, when you see others walking in their purpose being blessed with the favor of the Lord following them everywhere they go, you cannot handle it because you played with your purpose!

CHAPTER

3

Don't Go Back In The Room

LESSON

3

You can go in a room where it maybe legal in the natural, but illegal in the spirit, especially when you do not have a covenant and you belong to the Lord. Nonetheless, if you decide to go back in the room, then what happened to you might be found out – from being in the room. Ultimately, you may enter the room wearing clothes in the natural, but you will leave the room spiritually naked.

For he that soweth to his flesh shall of the flesh reap corruption; but he that soweth to the Spirit shall of the Spirit reap life everlasting.
Galatians 6:8 (KJV)

The one who sows to please his sinful nature, from that nature will reap destruction; the one who sows to please the Spirit, from the Spirit will reap eternal life.
Galatians 6:8 (NIV)

The person who plants selfishness, ignoring the needs of others –Ignoring God! – harvests a crop of weeds. All he'll have to show for his life is weeds!
Galatians 6:8 (MSB)

If he sows to please his own wrong desires, he will be planting seeds of evil and he will surely reap a harvest of spiritual decay and death; but if he plants the good things of the Spirit, he will reap the everlasting life which the Holy Spirit gives him.
Galatians 6:8 (TLB)

If Jesus couldn't go in the room, then why did I walk through the door? I didn't expect a disease to be the result from being in the room. When it was all over, nothing good came from it. I was only left with hurt, sin, sickness and shame. Why did I open the door? Why did I go in the room?

Hence, this is what happens when the lord gives you a word, "Don't go back in the room!"

You can go in a room where it maybe legal in the natural, but illegal in the spirit, especially when you go in a room without a covenant and you belong to the Lord. However, if you decide to go back in the room, then what happened to you might be found out – from being in the room. Ultimately, you may enter the room wearing clothes in the natural, but you will leave the room spiritually naked.

With that being said, I was holding on to the Word of the Lord and remaining celibate. As time passed by and my loneliness begin to take over as well as other frustrations and distractions that came my way, I let my guard down from what appeared to be harmless conversations and laughter. Nevertheless, all of the demonic distractions were only sent as a strategic setup to pull me into the room, contaminate my vessel with the smell of sin and shipwreck my destiny!

With consistency and strategic words, the enemy used everything he could. He was on a mission. That is why the Bible says in the first part of the scripture in John 10:10, *"The thief cometh not, but for to steal, and to kill, and to destroy!"* With the right words and a hard season full of frustrations and financial hardships – my heart slowly was pried opened. **The definition of the word pry is to get, to move, to separate, to**

unlock something, to pull something open by force and open by leverage. The enemy was not only after my relationship with my Lord and Savior and my purpose, but he was definitely after my prayer life. In I Chronicles 16:11, the Bible illustrates, *"Look to the Lord and His strength; seek his face always."*

Prayer has always been one of the most important priorities in my life as well as my love language towards the Lord. For me, prayer was always the first thing I did in the morning, during day, before I went to bed and throughout the night. It has always been my lifeline.

I prayed all the time without ceasing. In 1 Thessalonians 5:17, the Word of God says, *"You should continually pray without ceasing!"* At that time, with a decrease in my prayer life, I felt naked and disconnected from the Lord. When I stopped praying and seeking the face of the Lord, everything that guarded my heart and my life was now off. I put my season with the Lord up for auction and my soul in jeopardy.

Gradually, my routine changed. Prayer became less and less and even my desire to pray. The voice of God grew farther away from the core of my heart. It was no one else's fault, but my own. Although the Lord sent His warning, I turned my heart to a place where I could find dangerous rest, fulfill fleshly desires and fill the void of loneliness in my heart.

Thus, with a silent conviction in my heart, I eventually walked the plank of sin and went into the room. I found myself in the room where sin was waiting to explode and sickness and death signed a contract to purchase my life and to destroy my purpose.

Since I was in the room, I was putting my season with the Lord in jeopardy and my destiny on hold because of my disobedience and acting like – a silly woman. ***The word silly*** *means to lack in good sense, to be superficial, weak in intellect or weak minded. It means to live a low life and to have little to no respect for yourself. Furthermore, a silly woman is a woman who has a heart open to anyone who walks by, easily flattered, enjoys worldly pleasure, easy prey for the enemy to distract her, pulls her away from the things of God and overtakes her mentally and emotionally because of the weakness of her mind and desires of her flesh.* The Word of God reads it like this, *"For of this sort are they which creep into houses and lead captive silly women laden with sins, lead away with divers lusts.* 2 Timothy 3:6 (KJV)

There was nothing in the room good for me to receive or do – except for me to leave. After it was all over, I left the room not by choice and went home. Immediately, I ran into my closet, fell on my face and cried out to the Lord for what I did to my vessel and my covenant with the Lord. I was naked and totally ashamed. I disappointed my Lord. In the end, all I obtained was temporary satisfaction with long term pains.

The room was the last place I should have been, unless I was in the room by myself, with my family or spending time with the Lord. That was not the case, however. Consequently, this was a decision made by the lust of the flesh (*what I wanted*), the lust of the eyes (*what I saw*) and the pride of life *(what I desired to do)*. In all honesty, without a covenant – the only thing available in the room is a spiritual or physical death sentence given by the enemy. Nonetheless, I ended up doing what I chose. I paid the consequences for being in a relationship of convenience rather than being in a covenant. A few moments of false affections and misleading promises–cost me condemnation, embarrassment, humiliation and shame.

On a sunshiny day, I called the person who was in the room with me. Almost immediately, once I communicated with him after what happened in the room, he laughed at me. His laughter sounded like it came from the camp of the enemy. I felt like a fool and burst into tears.

I should not have been upset with him especially when the Lord sent me a warning and I still proceeded to have a relationship and go in the same direction where the Lord told me not to go. It was my fault. It not only turned into the fight of my life, but one of the biggest mistakes of my life. I will live with that regret – for the rest of my life.

As time passed by and the season finally changed, I learned valuable lessons I vowed to teach others. If you are not in the room out of a covenant, you are going for convenience, especially when you are going to satisfy the flesh! When you make that choice, you choose to put your destiny on hold and destroy your purpose! That is one defeat that takes place when you go back in the room!

What would make you go to a place which represents spiritual darkness and worldly deception anyway? Why would you prefer convenience over a covenant? That is what the enemy offers! If you take the bait, the enemy will use that bait to destroy you!

Therefore, if it looks like the enemy, then it is! He or she may come to you in a different season, but it will be the same spirit!!!He or she will always present a relationship that appears to be going in the direction of a covenant, but it will only be a relationship of convenience that will slowly confiscate – your destiny! Just remember, it will never include a covenant! Remember, the Word of God states in John 10:10,

"*The enemy comes to kill, steal and destroy!*" The enemy comes to offer you temporary convenience – but not a permanent covenant! Without a permanent covenant, you will stay uncovered! When you are uncovered, you are available to every trap, setup and deception of the enemy! That is why you always need a covenant in a relationship. That is what Jesus always offers. Jesus is all about covenant. ***The definition of a covenant is an agreement, a contract, a commitment, a pledge, a promise, or a guarantee between God and His People.*** Do you have a covenant? Is your covenant with the world? Or is your covenant with Jesus? His covenant does not leave a lasting feeling of shame, guilt or condemnation. However, a covenant with the world will leave you empty, feeling used and perhaps keep you going back in the room!

Honestly, the enemy loves for you to be invited in a room, such as–a hotel room or a bedroom, specifically when you do not have a covenant with the person in the room! When it is all over, the enemy uses that same room to destroy your name, your reputation, your self-esteem, your self-worth, and even give you a lifelong disease after your enjoyment from being in the room!

Do you understand the dangers of those words the Lord gave me, "Don't Go Back In The Room!" Because what happens to you in the room does not always stay in room! Often times, what happened to you in the room, may not be found out until nine months later or years later, depending on what happened in the room! How many times have you participated in a relationship of convenience which required you to go back in the room? How many times have you gone in a room where you knew Jesus was there with you, but you ignored the conviction from the Holy Spirit for you to leave the room? When you ignore the words from the Lord that you should not be in the room, then you give the enemy a special invitation to be in the room with you! When you make this choice, the enemy will watch you, play with you and eventually do his best to destroy you! ***Remember, he is coming to destroy your name, kill you in the spirit and in the natural and eliminate your destiny!***

Therefore, when you decide to go in a room, Jesus should be able to go in the room with you! I found in life, unless my Savior is invited in the room, then I will not participate in simple room convenience, but only a covenant. Remember, Jesus came so you would have a right to a true covenant, but not something which offers you a temporary convenience. If someone ask you to go in the room, you need to make sure you ask the person, "Will Jesus be going in the room with us?" If Jesus cannot go in the room, you should not go in the room either! The Word of the Lord declares specifically in Revelation 3:20-21, *Behold! I stand at the door, and knock: If anyone hears my voice, and open the door, I will come in to him, and will sup with him, and he with me. To him that overcometh will I grant to sit with me in my throne, even as I also overcame, and am set down with my Father in His throne.*(KJV) In this text, Jesus is knocking at the door. He wants to come in the room.

Will you give Him an invitation to come into the most important room in your life – which is your heart and soul? Jesus wants to love you, protect you and show you your purpose and assignment, so that the only rooms or doors you walk through for the rest of your life will have Jesus attached to it. If you do it His way and follow the steps He has assigned for you, then He will never have to send you a warning. In conclusion, when you discover you cannot invite Jesus in the room where there is no covenant then – ***don't go back in the room!***

CHAPTER 4

Something About Momma

LESSON

4

When a Momma sees her child in trouble, she will call on the Lord for an answer and then pray until it comes. That is what a real Momma does.

He went in therefore, and shut the door upon them twain, and prayed unto the Lord. And he went up, and lay upon the child...and he stretched himself upon the child; and the flesh of the child waxed warm.
2 Kings 4:33-34 (KJV)

*He went in, shut the door on the two of them and prayed to the Lord. Then he got on the bed and lay upon the boy...as he stretched himself out upon him,
the boy's body grew warm.*
2 Kings 4:33-34 (NIV)

He went into the room and locked the door, just the two of them in the room, and prayed to God. He then got into the bed with the boy...As he was stretched out over him like that, the boy's body became warm.
2 Kings 4:33-34 (MSB)

He went in and shut the door behind him and prayed to the Lord. Then he lay upon the child's body...And the child's body began to grow warm again!
2 Kings 4:33-34 (TLB)

Momma told me she always knows when something is wrong with one of her children. On that day, there was something wrong with me. Her eyes wanted to fix it, but she prayed for me instead.

This day was like no other. I was so ill. Something I never sensed was coming after me. In my body, hell and the spirit of death was unleashed against me. As sick as I was, I had to make it to Momma's house.

As I was driving very fast down, I-10, I was praying to the Lord I would get there real soon. My body was out of order. Whatever was happening to me, I realized quickly it was not good. This thing sent from hell – was trying to take me out.

Before long, I arrived at Momma's house and ran to the bathroom with the little strength I had. I was shaking and my body was fighting within itself. The fight started, but the war was far from over.

Initially, I thought I was going to vomit because my stomach was churning in every direction. However, it was only the beginning of the war. There was more. I dropped down swiftly on the toilet seat and whatever was in my stomach came out. I had diarrhea at first. Soon following, the diarrhea turned – to brown water.

Then all of a sudden, without even realizing it, I was throwing up and releasing the brown water from my bottom – at the same time. Everything was on a towel as well as on the floor. My body was shaking and trembling. I had no idea what was wrong. At the time, I thought to myself, *"Something is trying to kill me!"*

When I finished, I sat on the toilet quivering. I emptied out all of the food, all of the nutrients and all of the waste in my bowels. I felt as if nothing was left.

After I was done, I went to my Momma's room and told her I was sick. However, I did not know what it was. My body was out of order. I felt like death was close by me. I did not have a lot of strength, not even enough to pray for myself.

I remember I called Momma to come into the room and pray for me. She saw I was trembling. She looked at me and recited the Psalm 23 which states, *"The Lord is my Shepherd; I shall not want...."* After that, she lay her body across mine like it illustrates in 2 Kings 4:33-34, *"He went in therefore, and shut the door upon them twain (two), and prayed unto the Lord. And he went up, and lay upon the child..."* (KJV)

In a few minutes, peace came and the trembling stopped. She remained in the room for a while until she thought I was okay. The prayer she prayed that night kept me once more. My body was exhausted from the internal fight which took place earlier in the bathroom. However, one thing I knew for sure was on that particular night – the death angel left the room.

There is something about my Momma. She not only spoke a word, but she released it into the atmosphere. After she prayed, the enemy left the room and my strength slowly returned to my body. That is what happened when my Momma prayed.

CHAPTER 5
Something Is Wrong

LESSON

5

If something is wrong in your body, normally there are signs which are speaking to you. You may not want to know what they are, but the warnings are there so you can find out the truth. For it is the truth that will set you free – one way or the other.

And a woman having an issue of blood twelve years, which had spent all her living upon physicians, neither could be healed of any.
Luke 8:43 (KJV)

And a woman was there who had been subject to bleeding for twelve years, but no one could heal her.
Luke 8:43 (NIV)

In the crowd that day there was a woman who for twelve years had been afflicted with hemorrhages. She had spent every penny she had on doctors but not one had been able to help her.
Luke 8:43 (MSB)

As they went a woman who wanted to be healed came up behind and touched him, for she had been slowly bleeding for twelve years, and could find no cure.
Luke 8:43 (TLB)

Its not always the beautiful things you and I have done that will pull people out of a dark place. Most of the time, it is the ugly, dark and sinful events in our lives that will change, transform, save a lost soul and pull them out of the pit.

It was a beautiful afternoon. As I recall, I decided to go for an afternoon jog. I always loved exercising and running. So, without much thought, I put on my jogging shoes and started my run. Surprisingly, when I finished, I was extremely tired and sort of out of breathe as if I had not run in years.

It was strange for me because I never had any breathing problems or challenges with my lungs. For the most part, I have always been healthy. Naturally, I did not understand what was happening. For sure, something was wrong.

My bones were aching. I had a high level of discomfort all over my body. Honestly, it did not sit too well with me because I was always careful about taking care of my physical health and anything pertaining to my body. Whatever this was, I knew it was not good. I was in pain all over.

As the day went by, I had intense shooting pains go all the way up my legs and up and down my back. The shooting pains were so severe they brought tears to my eyes. I remember I was sitting in my chair in the living room thinking maybe I ran too hard or too long, but the discomfort I was subjected to had nothing to do with running. This was something else. As much as I tried to ponder what it was, no answer or thought came close.

I knew this strange thing which came upon me was more than I could grasp. Almost immediately, my thoughts drifted in places such as, maybe it could be this or maybe it could be that. As time went by, my peace begin to slowly leave my heart. That is why the word of God says in Philippians 4:7, *"And the peace of God which passeth all understanding, shall keep your hearts and mind through Christ Jesus."* (KJV) Momentarily, I tried to put my mind on Christ Jesus and somehow keep my heart in a place of peace.

While I was struggling keeping peace in my heart and mind, I decided to call my mother to see how she was enjoying her day. Before our conversation went too far, I remember her telling me specifically, *"You need to go to the doctor!" "You need to go now!"* However, I had not told my mother I was having shooting pains in my body or extreme discomfort in my bones.

So, I was thinking to myself, *"How did she know to tell me that?"* Then, as I sat there, I knew the Lord was telling me through my mother I needed to go to the doctor as soon as possible. By this time, I recognized the pains increased from bad to worse, including severe throbbing headaches.

The throbbing pains from the headaches were in areas in my head where medicine did not even reach. I attempted to take an Advil to quiet and slow down the pounding due to the headaches. Regardless, after several hours, nothing worked. The headaches grew worse and the intense stinging pain in my skin. I thought to myself, *"Something is definitely wrong!"*

I was experiencing extreme pains coming from various areas of my body by now. From that moment, the doctor visit was needed immediately. This was an emergency. I was sick.

Whatever this was, it was not going away. It was obvious. In my heart, I was already afraid of what my doctor might find. Though 2 Timothy reads, *"For God hath not given us the spirit of fear; but of power, and of love, and of a sound mind."* (KJV) Although this scripture was true, I allowed fear to invade my heart early without knowing what was really wrong. Nonetheless, I was determined to find out what was the problem, even if I was already experiencing a little fear.

CHAPTER 6

My Doctor Called

LESSON

6

Some phone calls you never expect to get. But, when you do, you remember exactly where you were and how the call interrupted your life and shifted your destiny forever.

The Lord is my light and my salvation, whom shall I fear?
The Lord is the strength of my life;
of whom shall I be afraid?
Psalm 27:1 (KJV)

The Lord is my light and my salvation, whom shall I fear?
The Lord is the stronghold of my life;
of whom shall I be afraid?
Psalm 27:1 (NIV)

Light, space, zest – that's God! So, with him on my side
I'm fearless, afraid of no one and nothing.
Psalm 27:1 (MSB)

The Lord is my light and my salvation, whom shall I fear?
When evil men come to destroy me,
they will stumble and fall.
Psalm 27:1 (TLB)

The day I received a phone call from my doctor, I thought about all of the things from my past. At that moment, I was hoping it was a call for the good things instead of the bad.

My doctor called. This was the day everything started. It was the moment which escorted me into the fight of my life. I did not recognize what kind of fight it would be. It arrived on my door step with my name attached to it. My fight was now– here.

I sure did not know what the fight would include and how long it would take. However, I found out soon. This is what happened. This is the truth. This was the day that changed my life.

I was on my way to my family reunion in New Orleans, Louisiana, riding along I-10 East. It was a beautiful picturesque day. The sky was a clear crystal blue. The sun was sitting perfectly in its usual place warming everything underneath its authority as it was designed to do by the purpose of God. The water on each side of the highway was quietly resting while enjoying the hot summer day.

As I was in expectation of another family gathering, I heard my phone ring. I had a flip phone at the time. It was not fancy. It was a very basic phone. Everything on the phone was generic as it came, even the ringer. The sound on the phone was not alarming, to say the least. However, I remember hearing it ring.

I did not immediately answer the phone because I was simply resting my mind while listening to the sound of the music and the joyful laughter echoing in the car. We were still in route to our family destination of annual fun and family excitement. I was on my way to my family reunion. I definitely did not want to miss the moments being shared.

Everything in the atmosphere seemed perfect. All of the words which were placed in sentences as well as the jokes were in total harmony with one another. Nothing appeared to be out of the place. My mind was at peace. My heart was at rest.

After a little while, I decided to check my voicemail to see who called me and what sort of message I received. Of course, I thought the message would be something which would fit the normal. I imagined it would be a friend or a family member letting me know the details of the reunion ahead. However, the message I received was quite different. It was not what I expected at all.

My doctor's office called me. The message left was to call the office immediately. I thought to myself, *"What was this about?"* I never received a call like this before. *"Why now?"* I thought quietly. I had only been sick a few times in my life, but I knew it. So, this was totally different. Why did I need to call the office? Was there an emergency I could not see?

Quite naturally, I instantly became nervous. My hands were shaking a little and my stomach was churning all at once. All I thought was, *"What could it be?" "What did the test results conclude?"* I knew I had not been to the doctor in a few years and had a proper checkup.

As time went by, I quickly tried to regroup. One thing I remembered was my doctor explained to me about being mindful of taking too many long soaking bathes and the possibility of getting vaginal infections, especially from bubbles in the bathtub. For sure, I realized I did not follow her advice all the time. In times past, I experienced a few of them from not following her instructions.

When I thought about it again, I felt a little relieved about what would be found on the test. At least, I tried to be calm, but my mind could not rest. I just could not do it. I discerned something else was on it. However, I did not know what it was. In my gut, I realized the news I was about to receive might be unusual, but probably nothing more than a change in my diet was needed, perhaps. Yet, I still had this bad feeling in my gut. I never experienced anything like this before. I tried to shake it off, but it was too hard. I could feel the weight and the symptoms of the unknown about to overtake me.

I was definitely afraid of what I might hear from my doctor because I had not had a physical checkup in a long time. I kept thinking what was it? Obviously, I already started to worry. It was as if a silent fear gripped my heart and the spirit of heaviness arrived.

By this time, I arrived at my family reunion, attempting to appear calm and somewhat happy. Still, without anyone noticing, the tears begin to fall. I tried to hide them quickly hoping no one would see, but the Lord was watching this entire thing unravel. He always watched over me, no matter where I was in my life. Good, bad or even ugly, He was always there with me. The Word of God states in the book of Hebrew 13:5, *"I will not leave you nor forsake you."* (KJV)

Nevertheless, I quickly found a spot to make a phone call. I needed prayer immediately. I decided to call my Pastor. My tears were now falling like heavy rocks full of sorrow and pain. They were falling uncontrollably. I definitely desired a word to help me keep my mind and my heart together because I was struggling with the possibility of what was going on in my body. I was having a hard time keeping my face and my emotions on the happy side.

I had to pull things together. I was trying my best to look normal and enjoy my family reunion for the next few days. All I had to do was get through Friday, Saturday and Sunday Morning and the reunion would be over. *"Only three days,"* I said to myself. But, this would be the longest three days of my life.

Nevertheless, my Pastor prayed for me without reservation. He told me not to worry and to simply calm down. He explained to me worrying about something when I was not sure what the results were would only make things worse. After he prayed, I felt much better. At least, as much as I could. As it is written in James 5:14, *"Is any sick among you? Let him call for the elders of the church; and let them pray over him, anointing him with oil in the name of the Lord."* (KJV)

Whatever the doctor had to tell me was on my mind. There was nothing I could do for the next few days, so I attempted to enjoy the festivities of my family reunion as much as I could. I tried to smile on the outside. But, I still had this knot on the inside of my stomach. Nonetheless, I had to wait. The waiting was hard. It seemed forever. It seemed like an eternity. Regardless, I had to wait until Monday morning. This was the time I could finally find out why my doctor called.

CHAPTER 7

I Remember That Day

LESSON

7

There are days you will always remember. Not because of what was done, but the words which were said. Words can carry a death sentence. However, the right words can lead you to your destiny and ultimately your deliverance.

For I acknowledge my transgressions: and my sin is ever before me. Against thee, thee only, have I sinned and done this evil in thy sight: that thou mightiest be justified when you speakest, and be clear when you judgest.
Psalm 51:3-4 (KJV)

For I know my transgressions, and my sin is always before me. Against you, you only, have I sinned and done what is evil in your sight, so that you are proved right when you speak and justified when you judge.
Psalm 51:3-4 (NIV)

I know how bad I've been; my sins are staring me down. You're the One I've violated, and you've seen it all, seen the full extent of my evil. You have all the facts before you; whatever you decide about me is fair.
Psalm 51:3-4 (MSB)

For I admit my shameful deed – it haunts me day and night. It is against you and you alone I sinned, and did this terrible thing. You saw it all, and your sentence against me is just.
Psalm 51:3-4 (TLB)

Words have always carried power, whether in the mind or everyday life. Regardless of how they affect you, they will shift your life for that day or for the rest of your destiny.

I remember that day. I remember that day all so well. My appointment at my doctor's office was here. I was nervous and tensions were high. Before I left the house, I called and confirmed my appointment time just to be sure.

Unfortunately, I soon discovered my original doctor's appointment was not until Tuesday morning. There was no way possible I could wait that long. As a result, I made an appointment on Monday morning with another doctor who was available to give me the results on the report.

In a way, I was relieved to know I was about to find out the whole truth, whatever the truth maybe. I was on the verge of knowing what thing haunted me the last couple of days. The last few days was a quiet nightmare haunting my mind, my heart and my soul – both day and night!

I prepared myself as much as possible. I remember I told myself, *"Just take the Lord with you."* Based on the scripture in Deuteronomy 4:31, 35, *"For the Lord thy God is a merciful God, He will not forsake thee, neither destroy thee, nor forget the covenant of thy fathers which he sware unto them."* In verse 35 it says, *"Unto thee it was shewed, that thou mightiest know that the Lord he is God; there is none else beside him."* (KJV)

As I drove to the doctor's office, my mind went in different directions emotionally. I thought about my past and the events and toxic relationships which took place in my life. It seemed like my mind did a personal visitation of the past, especially because I was not sure if it was going to be positive.

I walked into the doctor's office. I sat in the chair like I normally would for any of my appointments. This time I was expecting a different doctor to speak with me. However, a nurse walked in the room instead. She appeared to be professional and kind. As she sat down, she went straight to the report.

While I sat in the chair, she asked me, *"Are you Elizabeth Perkins?"* I responded, *"Yes, of course."* Do you live at this current address? I stated, *"Yes, I do."* She begin to read the report to me and mentioned the things on the report that were negative. All I hoped was the doctor visit would be over sooner than later.

Then, all of sudden she paused and the atmosphere in the room was quiet. Without further ado, she told me I had a yeast infection. Since I had those before, I did not panic. I sort of knew from taking too many sit bathes, of course this would occur. Right behind that statement she stated without pause, *"You also tested positive for HIV!"*

When she released those words, I was speechless. I sat there in disbelief and complete despair. I felt like my soul left the room and the building all together. Nevertheless, there I was. I did not know what to say. I could not say a word.

She stated, *"Right now your test results are indeterminate."* I asked her, *"What does that mean?"* She explained to me, *"You tested positive for HIV, but you need to come back in a few weeks in order to be tested again to determine if you have the disease."*

Afterwards, she told me to sit on top of the table in order for her to examine my body. It was then, the tears begin to fall.

Instead of me wiping them away, I let them fall according to their own free will. It was all I could do. After a few minutes passed, all I thought about was how I would tell my family, how I would live and mostly – how I disappointed the Lord.

One thing I remembered was the nurse thoroughly checked my body to determine what stage was the HIV. I did not know exactly what that meant, but I heard of things about HIV on television and other information I occasionally read in magazines from time to time. Still, I never contemplated I would one day have to read information on HIV for myself. Nonetheless, I was able to get dressed once the procedure was done.

As I talked with her still crying of course, I asked her, *"Am I going to die?"* She simply stated, *"We are all going to die at some point, but that is what happens when you have unprotected sex!"* She went on further and said, *"But, if I were you, I would not look up anything on the internet about HIV because it will probably cause you to worry and not sleep much."* Then she finally said, *"But, if you know how to pray, you better start praying!"*

Even though her temperament and the words she released at first brought uneasiness to the current situation, I stopped and thought about the last statement she made. She said, *"If you know how to pray, you better start praying!"* As gloomy as the circumstances looked, all I thought about was that word – prayer. **Prayer is defined as the ability to make an intentional, earnest request or desperate plea to God!** I realized I could pray to the Lord and perhaps He would hear my heart of repentance. In I John 5:14, the Word reiterates, *"And this is the confidence that we have in him that, if we ask anything according to his will, he heareth us."* (KJV)

I was praying the Lord would hear my cry. **Cry means to lay prostrate while making a loud sound, to plead, to have sorrow or to weep continuously until the situation is resolved or heard by God.** According to the Word of God, *"For we have not received the spirit of bondage again to fear; but ye have received the Spirit of adoption, whereby we cry, Abba, Father."* Romans 8:15(KJV) I needed to cry out to My Lord. The heaviness on my heart was more than I could carry.

I knew I could go and talk with my heavenly Father, regardless of what happened, how it happened and no matter how ugly it looked. *Just like Jesus stated in His Word, "Then He called his twelve disciples together, and gave them power and authority over all devils, and to cure diseases."* Luke 9:1 (KJV)

With that in mind, I had to reach my Pastor. He always walked in authority of casting out devils and healing the sick. This was an emergency He could handle as well as bear. I was one of his disciples and I was in the fight of my life. I could not fight this one by myself. It was too much for me to handle.

As I got in my car, I immediately started releasing as many scriptures as I could into the atmosphere. The scriptures were the only thing which held my mind together. I was crying. I was angry at myself. I was angry at the choice I made which brought me to this point. Every choice in life has a definite consequence, whether it is good or bad. Unfortunately, a choice I made brought me to this point.

Here I was. I realized I contracted HIV regardless of what the nurse stated the test results were. I looked up all of the symptoms and I had many of them. The evidence did not lie and my blood did not either.

The Fight of My Life!

Indeterminate Test Result

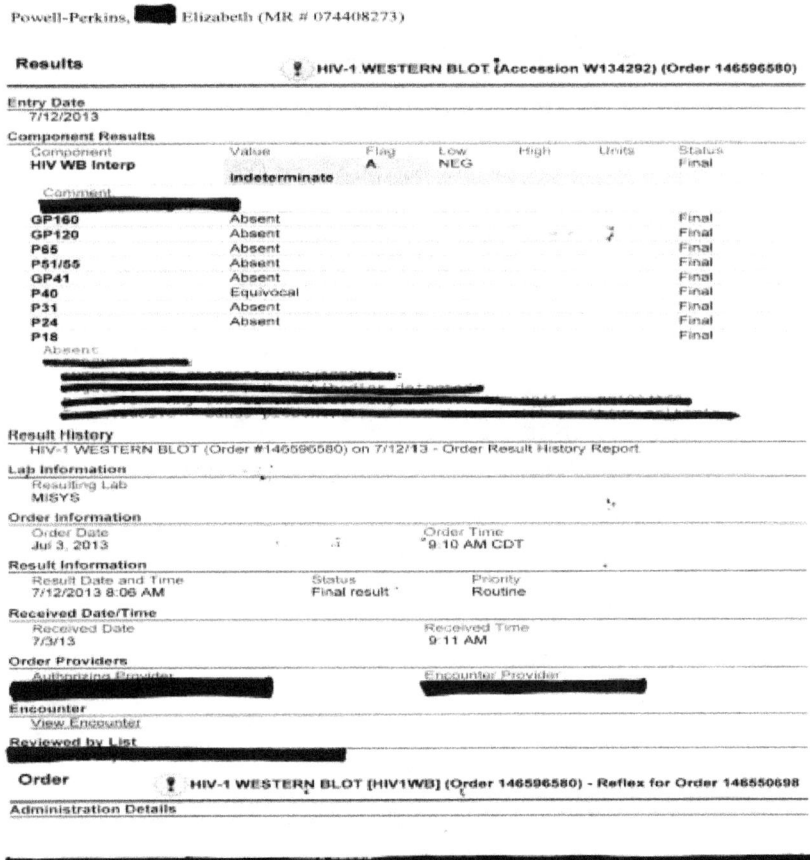

The indeterminate test result meant that the test results were not definite. Therefore, I had to return to the doctor to receive another blood test.

CHAPTER 8

When The Righteous Cry

LESSON

8

When the righteous cry out, the Lord not only hears them when they cry, but He remembers the sound and specific pain attached to the cry.

The righteous cry, and the Lord heareth, and delivereth them out of all their troubles.
Psalm 34:17 (KJV)

The righteous cry out, and the Lord hears them; he delivers them from all their troubles.
Psalm 34:17 (NIV)

Is Anyone Crying for help? God is listening, ready to rescue you.
Psalm 34:17 (MSB)

Yes, the Lord hears the good man when he calls to him for help, and saves him out of all his troubles.
Psalm 34:17 (TLB)

A cry is defined as a quiet or a loud turbulent sound out of despair or desperation. When I cried out to the Lord, I cried loudly because I was desperate and I felt death at my door.

When I walked in the door after returning from the doctor, I immediately ran to my bedroom, stretched out on the floor next to my bed and cried out to the Lord. The book of 2 Samuel 22:7, states, *"In my distress, I called upon the LORD, and cried unto my God: he heard my voice out of his temple, and my cry did enter into his ears."* (KJV) After I wailed for several hours that morning, I repented and begged the Lord for His forgiveness because of my disobedience.

With humility and a contrite heart, I told Him how sorry I was for committing a sin against my temple and against His Word. The Word says in Psalm 51:4, *"Against thee, thee only, have I sinned, and done this evil in thy sight: that thou mightiest be justified when thou speakest, and be clear when thou judgest."* (KJV)

Due to my defiance, the Lord had a right to judge me and deal with me according to what I had done as well as the outcome of me contracting HIV. As such, I pleaded with the Lord like Hezekiah did in the book of 2 Kings 20:1-2, *"In those days Hezekiah became ill and was at the point of death. The prophet Isaiah son of Amoz went to him and said, "This is what the Lord says: Put your house in order, because you are going to die; you will not recover." "Hezekiah turned his face to the wall and prayed to the Lord, Remember, Lord, how I have walked before you faithfully and with wholehearted devotion and have done what is good in your eyes." And Hezekiah wept bitterly.*(KJV)

While I was on the floor, I came clean with the Lord about the truth of the matter, although He had the details in His record book in heaven. Moreover, I expressed to the Lord I would pray for every soul I met, lay hands on the sick and walk in my ministry assignment, regardless of how I felt.

Furthermore, I made an agreement and a vow to the Lord if He healed me from HIV, I would tell the whole world of the miracle He performed. ***A vow is defined as a solemn promise, an oath or a pledge to do a specific thing.*** I promised to keep my vow, if I was healed of this dreadful condition. I was standing on the Word of God which says, *"And the prayer of faith shall save the sick, and the Lord shall raise him up; and if he have committed sins, they shall be forgiven him."* James 5:15 (KJV)

The Lord was my only hope and redeemer. Based on the Word of God, *Christ hath redeemed us from the curse of the law, being made a curse for us,* according to Galatians 3:13. (KJV) I was believing the Lord to heal me from this curse and blood condition no matter how long it would take. According to Jeremiah 29:17, the Bible says, *"For I will restore health unto thee, and I will heal thee of thy wounds, saith the Lord; because they called thee an Outcast, saying this is Zion, whom no man seeketh after."* (KJV)

I was in the fight of my life. Yet, I could not enter into this demonic territory of deliverance on my own. Soon after, I made this gross discovery, I knew I had to reach my Pastor. I was shattered, in addition to being full of deep shame and condemnation, although the bible states in John 3:17, *"For God sent not his Son into the world to condemn the world; but that the world through him might be saved."* (KJV)

With a heavy heart and tears streaming down my face, I called my Pastor regarding the news I received from the doctor. I explained to him I had some disturbing news the doctor gave me regarding the report. I definitely did not know what to say or how to say it, but I was already experiencing anxiety and even suicidal thoughts. I needed prayer for my mind and a word from the Lord.

So, I stated to him, *"The report from the doctor came back. According to the report, I tested positive for HIV."* I recognized in my heart, I was not equipped to deal with this shocking news. I wanted to fall apart. In return he replied, *"Are you ok?"*

Then he said, *"Where is your faith?"* Quite obviously, I had some faith, but the faith I carried was not enough to confront the news I received. At least, that is what I believed at the time. After that, he went on to say, *"Well, what about if we believe the Lord for a miracle?" "It would be an awesome testimony of God's healing power!" "Well, I know what to do. Let me go to the Lord in prayer on your behalf."* My response was, *"Okay."*

Of course, I was grateful. I was not relieved, however. All I stared at for several hours was the report from the doctor. I could not believe my name was on it. I was in total disbelief. I carried a disease in my blood called – HIV.

This was enough for me to end it all. But, then, if I ended my life, what would the Lord say to me when I saw His face? Would He ask me, *"Why didn't you believe?"* Instead, I was reminded of what my Pastor said to me on the phone before I hung up. He said, *"You will live and not die and declare the works of the Lord!"* I received those words as much as I could with tears slowly streaming down.

Nonetheless, I cried out to the Lord day and night. The Word states in Exodus 2:23, *"And it came to pass in process of time that the king of Egypt died: and the children of Israel sighed by reason of the bondage, and they cried, and their cry came up unto God by reason of the bondage."* (KJV) I was in bondage with HIV. Therefore, I cried out to the Lord. I cried out not just because I was desperate, but because I wanted to be set free.

*For God
Hath not given us
The spirit of fear;
But of power,
And of love,
And of a sound mind.*

—2 Timothy 1:7 (KJV)

Section 2

The Second Fight: Fighting For My Mind

CHAPTER

9

Whose Report Will You Believe?

LESSON

9

The words released over your life whether they are good or bad have the power to alter your thinking and the power to make you decide whose report will you believe?

Who hath believed our report? And to whom is the arm of the Lord revealed?
Isaiah 53:1 (KJV)

Who has believed our message and to whom has the arm of the Lord been revealed?
Isaiah 53:1 (NIV)

Who believes what we've heard and seen? Who would have thought God's saving power would look like this?
Isaiah 53:1 (MSB)

But, OH, How few believe it! Who will listen? To whom will God reveal His saving power?
Isaiah 53:1 (TLB)

When a statement or a report is given to you, you have to choose to believe it or not. If there is truth to it, you still have to make up your mind and be fully persuaded whose words will you believe?

I was required to return to the doctor for another blood test. I made sure I fasted the night before as required, but I also spent the night laying out before the Lord. All I desired was to be in the presence of the Lord. At this point, nothing else mattered. I longed for the Lord more than anything. I wanted to make everything right with Him.

My blood test was done. After this, I waited on the results. Of course, this was the hardest point. By this time anyway, the symptoms described with HIV were quite obvious. Be that as it may, when you have to wait on an HIV test result, your life and your plans flash before your eyes. Here I was – waiting along with flashbacks. *A flashback is defined as constant interruptions which take place in the mind from an event or a tragic episode that took place earlier in your life.*

The next day I received the results. I hoped what I felt in my body was false. However, the truth was out. The test results were positive. I had HIV in my bloodstream.

The report came back positive and the discomfort in my body agreed with it. What almost caused me total devastation was when the test results came back HIV1 and HIV2! The HIV2 was not treatable in this country. Both showed up in my blood test. When I received this news I believe I almost fainted. My heart was beating a thousand beats per minute. I was overwhelmed.

At this moment, all I thought about were three things. The warning the Lord sent me, the decision I made not to yield to the warning and the bad choice I made. These three areas cost me almost everything, including now – the fight of my life!

By this time, I left the doctor's office immediately. I put my shades on in order to avoid the appearance I was crying. Everything shifted. My life was up for auction by the enemy. In the Word it reiterates, *"And fear not them which kill the body, but are not able to kill the soul: but rather fear him which is able to destroy both soul and body in hell."* Matthew 10:28 (KJV)

In my mind and heart, I was desperate to get to church. It was imperative my Pastor see the paperwork which held the test results. It went from indeterminate to definite. This condition was in my bloodstream. It was evident and the days of sickness that accompanied it. By then, my sick days were more often than not.

I soon approached the church and knocked on the door. My Pastor answered. I believed when he saw my face he recognized the news I heard. While my hands were trembling, I removed the paperwork from my hand and gave it to him. I said," *The test results are positive."* "The HIV is in my bloodstream."

He quietly glanced at me with assurance and stated, *"Why are you crying?"* So, I responded, *"What is going to happen to me now?"* In the past, I heard so many stories of HIV and how many people died early. However, he looked at me and repeated, *"Where is your faith?"* *"Don't you know God is a miracle worker and you still belong to Him?"* "I realized the Word of God said in Jeremiah 1:5, *"Before I formed thee in the belly I knew thee."* (KVJ)

The Fight of My Life!

Once again, he directed me back to the Word of the Lord and as a result, he took out his oil, prayed for me and gave me scriptures to take home with me. I knew he believed in the power of healing and the power of prayer. I was going to have to do the same thing too. Prayer can change everything, especially if you believe. That day when I left the office, I only had one question in my heart whose report would– I believe?

Elizabeth Perkins

The First Test Result

Powell-Perkins, Elizabeth (MR # 074408273)

Results — HIV-1/HIV-2 ROUTINE SCREENING (Accession W134292) (Order 146550698)

Entry Date
7/12/2013

Component Results

Component	Value	Flag	Low	High	Units	Status
HIV-1/HIV-2	Positive	A	NEG			Final

Comment:
This is only a screening test. If the result is positive, HIV-1 Western Blot test will be performed to confirm the diagnosis of HIV-1 infection.

Result History
HIV-1/HIV-2 ROUTINE SCREENING (Order #146550698) on 7/12/13 - Order Result History Report.

Lab Information
Resulting Lab
MISYS

Order Information

Order Date	Order Time
Jul 3, 2013	9:10 AM CDT

Result Information

Result Date and Time	Status	Priority
7/12/2013 3:07 PM	Final result	Routine

Received Date/Time

Received Date	Received Time
7/3/13	9:11 AM

Order Providers

Authorizing Provider	Encounter Provider

Encounter
View Encounter

Reviewed by List

Order — HIV-1/HIV-2 ROUTINE SCREENING [HIVRUS] (Order 146550698)

Administration Details

Order Information

Order Date/Time	Release Date/Time	Start Date/Time	End Date/Time
7/3/2013 8:23 AM	7/3/2013 9:10 AM	7/3/2013	None

Order Details

Frequency	Duration	Priority	Order Class
None	None	Routine	Normal

Quantity

Ordering Quantity
1

Original Order

Ordered On	Ordered By
Wed Jul 3, 2013 8:23 AM	

The first test result was the test I received with HIV positive. After the results, my heart and soul were shattered.

CHAPTER 10

Is There Anything Too Hard For The Lord?

LESSON

10

There are things in life that will be too much for you to carry and too much for you to bear. Yet, there is nothing too hard for God. He can handle all of your tests, trials and tribulations. He can handle them all.

Behold, I am the Lord, the God of all flesh: is there anything too hard for me?
Jeremiah 32:27 (KJV)

I am the Lord, the God of all mankind. Is anything too hard for me?
Jeremiah 32:27 (NIV)

I am God, the God of everything living. Is there anything I can't do?
Jeremiah 32:27 (MSB)

I am the Lord, the God of all mankind; is there anything too hard for me?
Jeremiah 32:27 (TLB)

Whenever you are in trouble, no matter how bad it is, there is nothing too hard for God to handle. He will never leave you when others walk away. You can trust Him with everything, even with your tears.

The news I received from my doctor turned my life upside down. I was not prepared for it and how to live my everyday life, except to go and talk to the Lord. All I knew was this situation was over my head and over my level of faith. I did not know of anyone who had been healed from HIV, but I concluded in my heart, maybe the Lord could heal me? According to Psalm 34:18-19 the Word of God says, *"The Lord is nigh unto them that are of a broken heart; and saveth such as be of a contrite spirit. Many are the afflictions of the righteous: but the LORD delivereth him out of them all."* (KJV)

It was possible. Still, I was not close to being sure what outcome I would have in the upcoming months, years and perhaps the rest of my life. Nevertheless, I definitely wanted to believe there was nothing too hard for the Lord. I had to lean on the scripture that states, *"Behold, I am the Lord, the God of all flesh: is there anything too hard for me?"* Jeremiah 32:27 (KJV)

While everything slowly unraveled, I recognized this was too much for me to carry. Wholeheartedly, there are things in your life that will be too much for you to carry and too much for you to bear. Yet, there is nothing that is too hard for God. He can handle all of your tests, trials and tribulations. He can handle them all.

With tears falling down my face and disappointment in my heart, I sat on my sofa thinking about this long emotional day. This was a day I would never forget, especially hearing my name called with the bad news I received. I remember it was a sunny day outside, but I was too emotionally fragile to venture out anywhere. Too afraid to call anyone, I went to my bedroom and sat on my bed.

I kept thinking, *"What am I going to do now?" "How could I have allowed myself to be in this kind of situation?"* Then I thought, *"Would the Lord still receive my prayers?" "Would He receive my repentance?"* Would He hear my cry?"

A number of thoughts crossed my heart. I fell on the floor and cried out to the Lord even the more when I imagined the HIV being in my blood stream. As the Word of God reads in Psalm 27:7, "*Hear, O, Lord, when I cry with my voice: have mercy also upon me, and answer me.*" (KJV)

Maybe, the Lord could give me a supernatural blood transfusion? *"Was that even possible?"* I thought to myself. I attempted to rest on the floor for a while. The only thing I desired was to find a place where I could lay out before the Lord. I tried my best to contain my tears because it was so many of them. I read Psalm 18:6 often, which says "*In my distress I called upon the Lord, and cried unto my God: he heard my voice out of his temple, and my cry came before Him, even into his ears.*" (KJV)

Although I caused this trial to come upon me, I held on to the strength of the Lord. "*The Lord is my light and my salvation; whom shall I fear? The Lord is the strength of my life; of whom shall I be afraid, according to Psalm 27:1.*" (KJV)

My thoughts were going in every direction. If I did not allow my tears to come down and release the scream in my soul, I possibly would have hurt myself. The embarrassment and the shame took me to a place where I almost forgot the Lord is still a healer. But, what would I believe?

That is where I was. I was now contaminated. Nevertheless, I reminded myself of what my Pastor told me before I left the church, *"There is nothing too hard for the Lord."* Just like the scripture reads in Psalm 24:8, *"Who is this King of glory? The Lord strong and mighty, the Lord mighty in battle."* (KJV) He was still my Lord and my King of Glory. As far as I was concerned, I had to trust the Lord and His Word. I had to trust Him to keep me until this fight of my life had a conclusion and a different result at the end. Nevertheless, I had to have the patience like the Woman with the issue of blood and wait on the Lord.

CHAPTER 11

The Waiting Room

LESSON

11

The waiting room is the room where God speaks to you and teaches you about lessons in life while you are fighting for your life. It is in this room where you have to pass your spiritual lessons and physical lessons in order to find out if you will be delivered and what words the Lord will finally say to you.

Yea, though I walk through the valley of the shadow of death, I will fear no evil: for thou art with me; thy rod and thy staff they comfort me.
Psalm 23:4 (KJV)

Even though I walk through the valley of the shadow of death, I will fear no evil, for you are with me; your rod and your staff, they comfort me.
Psalm 23:4 (NIV)

Even when the way goes through Death Valley, I'm not afraid when you walk at my side. Your trusty shepherd's crook makes me feel secure.
Psalm 23:4 (MSB)

Even when walking through the dark valley of death I will not be afraid, for you are close behind me, guarding, guiding all the way.
Psalm 23:4 (TLB)

There are certain things that cannot be rushed, hurried or prayed through quickly. That is why it is called the waiting room. It is in this place where you have to be patient, loving, kind, gentle and have faith while you are waiting.

After the initial shock was over and the results were positive, I sat in – the waiting room. At first, I did not understand what was the purpose of this room? As time passed, I recognized the waiting room was a room which housed life lessons I had to learn. There were spiritual lessons and physical lessons while I sat in the waiting room. The Lord was the instructor and I was the student. I wanted to be His disciple all over again.

Hence, I believe in my heart the spiritual lessons were to see and determine what kind of attitude I had towards the Lord while I was fighting HIV. *Would I blame Him for not protecting me against the sin I committed in His sight after He sent me a final warning? Would I blame Him for not allowing His grace to cover me from the assault against my vessel and His Word? Would I still worship Him in the beauty of His holiness? Or, would I keep my mouth closed because judgment arrived at my front door and now I was pleading with Him for His mercy?*

Thus, the spiritual lessons consisted of waiting to hear and see what the answer from the Lord would be. The verdict from the Lord had not arrived as of yet. Still, I had to wait in this place for the physical lessons as well. The physical lessons were to determine how I treated others while I waited. *Would I be judgmental towards others who had an issue, condition or a disease? How would I treat others who fell from their assignment?*

How would I treat others who ignored the final warning which came from the Lord? Would I look at them as if they should have been stronger or wiser? Or would I render them grace and mercy like I desired the Lord to give to me? Or could I use this sinful tragedy to help remind others the Lord is still full of mercy, if you truly repent and believe Him to forgive you?

The waiting room was not just a room for lessons to be taught, but tests to be passed also. Would I pass the Lord's test while I was in His waiting room? Would I understand the greatest commandment in the Word of God that Jesus stated in Matthew 22:37-39, *"Thou shalt love the Lord thy God with all thy heart, and with all thy soul, and with all thy mind." This is the first and great commandment. And the second is like unto it, Thou shalt love thy neighbor as thyself."* (KJV) I had to pass my tests.

In reality, the only two people in the waiting room was the Lord and myself. I was the woman with the condition and issue of blood. He was my Lord, Savior and even the Judge. After I my stay in the waiting room, the Lord would be the one to give me my passing grade. If not, my stay in the waiting room could be permanent.

I believe I went through the waiting room in order to get to the next area of deliverance in my life which was not just from the disease, but even from areas in my heart that only the Lord could see. That is why the Bible says, *"Man looks at the outer appearance, but the Lord looks straight at the heart."* I Samuel 16:7 (KJV)

I prayed to be healed from HIV, but also I desired deliverance from the strongholds which accompanied it, such as wrong desires and a wrong thought life. I was reminded all the time – they were not leaving without a fight.

The Fight of My Life!

I remember not too long after I found out what I was carrying, I attended a Women's Conference. As I sat in the car waiting to come into the conference, I briefly went on the internet to look at the reviews of how long people lived with HIV and what they went through physically and emotionally. All I remember was trying to pull myself together to look like I was well and whole, at least in front of the women at the conference.

I recognized I lost some weight. My appetite was poor, my confidence was at an all-time low and my attention span was non-existent. On many days, something on my body always hurt or either throbbed. Frankly, dealing with the pain in public was as difficult as it was in private.

I tried to live as pleasant as I could while battling this condition. So, I tried my best to act polite and look enthused about the meeting, although I would have preferred to be at home. It is easier to deal with pain in the privacy of your own home rather than dealing with it in the public eye, but I reminded myself the Lord was with me.

Nevertheless, I told myself, no matter how I felt, I would be focused on lifting up any woman that passed my way. I thought to myself, if I could keep my mind off of my condition, then maybe I could encourage someone else. It definitely was not the fault of any woman at the conference I had HIV. So, there was no reason for me to walk around bitter or angry.

In this place – I called the waiting room, I was determined to work on my internal attitude and get rid of any pride, arrogance, harshness or unforgiveness I carried consciously or unconsciously in my heart. I welcomed the

Lord with full permission to cut anything off my flesh that would hinder me from receiving my deliverance while I was in the room. The Lord had my complete cooperation. With total submission to Him, I took my seat in this room, while I allowed Him to stand up in His seat of authority as Lord, Master and of course, My Father.

As I lived in the waiting room, Monday through Sunday, the Lord allowed me to learn valuable lessons about life or else I would have lived there even longer. Although I walked through the valley of the shadow of death, His rod and His protection comforted me while I lived there. I always kept the scripture Psalm 23: 1-6 in my heart, *"The Lord is my shepherd; I shall not want. He maketh me lie down in green pastures: he leadeth me beside still waters. He restoreth my soul…surely goodness and mercy shall follow me all the days of my life: and I will dwell in the house of the LORD forever."* (KJV)

The Lord reminded me He was with me, whether through a scripture or a word of healing from my Pastor. I told the Lord I did not mind waiting as long as – He waited with me. Though I was waiting on my supernatural healing, I was waiting no matter what I had to go through in order to be healed.

CHAPTER 12

The Battle In My Mind

LESSON

12

When there is a battle in your mind, either fear, depression and defeat will take you over or deliverance will set you free. The choice is easy, but the process is hard.

For God hath not given us the spirit of fear; but of power, and of love, and a sound mind.
2 Timothy 1:7 (KJV)

For God did not give us a spirit of timidity, but a spirit of power, of love and of self-discipline.
2 Timothy 1:7 (NIV)

God doesn't want us to be shy with his gifts, but bold and loving and sensible.
2 Timothy 1:7 (MSB)

For the Holy Spirit, God's gift, does not want you to be afraid of people, but to be wise and strong, and to love them and enjoy being with them.
2 Timothy 1:7 (TLB)

The battle in your mind can either be won or lost. It actually depends on what you put in it and what you give away. Nevertheless, if you want to win the battle be prepared not just for a battle – but for war.

One of the greatest fights I endured while fighting for my life was – the battle in my mind. From the day I learned I had HIV, everything changed and so did all of my thoughts. The battle included not only my mind, but my will and my emotions. The enemy attempted to give me an emotional cardiac arrest. This is when the mind shuts down, emotions become numb, anxiety takes over and all you can feel is a faint beat of the heart.

I remember the day I left the doctor's office, I immediately arrested the negative thoughts and words which came from my mind. I made sure I spoke the Word of God over my life while I was driving. I quoted scriptures I carried in my heart. I released as many scriptures as possible.

Moreover, I repeated the power scriptures my Pastor stated during Sunday services. I released scripture after scripture and any encouraging quote I heard while at church. I spoke it over and over while my heart was racing a thousand beats per minute. Still, within a matter of a few hours, the battle in my mind turned from trying to speak right words to warfare. It was not just a battle, it was spiritual war. I never faced a battle such as this kind. All my mind focused on was – I had HIV. *What was I going to do? What would happen to me? Would I be sick the rest of my life? Am I going to die? How are you going to believe the Lord will heal you?*

As much as I attempted to take authority over how I felt, thoughts in my mind started to lean towards the areas which included shame, dirtiness, guilt, depression and especially fear. Based on the Word of God, *"The carnal mind is enmity against God: for it is not subject to the law of God, neither indeed can be."* Romans 8:7 (KJV) The battle for my mind and the thoughts I carried were now being tested for the trials I now faced. The Bible reads in James 1:2-3, *"My brethren, count it all joy when ye fall into divers temptations; knowing this, that the trying of your faith worketh patience,"* I realized I had faith, but not the kind of faith to be put on trial. At least, not yet.

While I sat on my sofa in order to pull my emotions together and to give my eyes a rest from crying, the pain in my body was on the rise, but the battle in my mind was rising quicker. When there is a battle in your mind, either fear, depression and defeat will take you over or deliverance will set you free. The choice is easy, but the process is hard. The process for me was not only hard, but it was extremely hard.

As such, that is why it is necessary to renew your mind every day in the Word. The Word of God states, *"And be not conformed to this world: but be ye transformed by the renewing of your mind, that ye may prove what is that good, and acceptable, and perfect, will of God."* Romans 12:2 (KJV) If you do not keep your mind renewed by the Word of God, the enemy will take over your mind by the cares and concerns of this world. He will try to consume your mind.

To be honest, the first thing which attempted to consume my mind was – fear. The spirit of fear tried to set in quickly and take over my mind as soon as I heard the words – "You tested positive for HIV!" Although the Word of God states,

The Fight of My Life!

"*God has not given us a spirit of fear....,*" I could feel the spirit of fear as if I could touch it. 2 Timothy 1:7 (KJV) The only thing in front of me was – fear.

For a time, it seemed as if my fear was increasing and my faith was decreasing. Initially, I felt powerless on many days and nights. It was a battle in my mind almost every day. Each time I reviewed the test results, all I saw was a woman who had HIV.

All I saw was a woman whose blood was contaminated and who carried HIV with her wherever she went. I was a contaminated vessel. Yet, I still loved the Lord with all of my heart, all of my mind and all of my soul. According to Deuteronomy 6:5, the Bible says, **"***And thou shalt love the Lord thy God with all thine heart, and with all thy soul, and with all thy might.***"**

During a few months, I remember sitting on my couch in my bedroom in a fetal position with my lights off. As the tears fell, my mind shifted to thoughts which were very dark and harmful to my faith. I believe there were one or two moments I wished I was not alive. Fear, powerlessness and the battle in my mind – took me over.

The battle in my mind included questions such as, "*How could you do that?*" "*What were you thinking?*" "*You are supposed to be a Woman of God?*" "*How could you do this to God?*" "*Do you think the Lord will ever forgive you?*" So many questions and thoughts of conviction rested on my mind almost every day of the week.

At first, there were periods when I wanted to commit spiritual suicide. **Spiritual suicide is when the enemy launched an all-out assault and attack against my mind – so that I would walk away from my assignment and particularly the Lord.** The enemy wanted me to think to myself, "*You are not *good enough to be a Christian!" "Look at what you have done!" "How can you preach the Gospel now?" "Who will listen to what you have to say!"* There were times when the battle went from bad to worse.

As a result, I told my Pastor about the struggle and the battle I was fighting in my mind. I remember when he told me, *"You still have an assignment! "You have to fight the enemy with the Word of God!" You can't go by what you feel! You are going to have to believe God for your healing by faith!"* I never realized the battle would be fought by the words I released from my mouth and ultimately– my faith!

He also reminded me to recite this scripture over and over – according to Philippians 4:8, *"Finally brethren, whatsoever things are true, whatsoever things are honest, whatsoever things are just, whatsoever things are pure, whatsoever things are lovely, whatsoever things are of a good report; if there be any virtue, and if there be any praise, think on these things!"* I had to remember those words to encourage myself.

I also had to remember the scripture the Lord told Joshua, *"Have not I commanded thee? Be strong and of a good courage; be not afraid, neither be thou dismayed: for the Lord thy God is with thee whithersoever thou goest."* Joshua 1:9 (KJV) These scriptures were not only necessary, but they were mandatory. I was fighting for my life.

I had to keep myself encouraged whether I wanted to or not. In fact, courage became my daily food from the Word of God, especially if I wanted to stay in the battle for the fight of my life. The enemy wanted to throw me overboard in the spirit, but I was determined to defeat him with the Word of God and not to let him win the battle. God was still God. He was still on His throne.

CHAPTER 13

The Battle In My Body

LESSON 13

If you ever had a battle in your body, there are two things you will always remember: the pain you endured and the prayers you prayed.

The Fight of My Life!

Have mercy upon me, O Lord; for I am weak: O Lord, heal me; for my bones are vexed. My soul is also sore vexed: but thou, O Lord, how long?
Psalm 6:2-3 (KJV)

Be merciful to me, Lord, for I am faint; O Lord, heal me, for my bones are in agony. My soul is in anguish. How long, O Lord, how long?
Psalm 6:2-3 (NIV)

Can't you see I'm black and blue, beat up badly in bones and soul? God, how long will it take for you to let up?
Psalm 6:2-3 (MSB)

Pity me, O Lord, for I am weak. Heal me, for my body is sick, and I am upset and disturbed. My mind is filled with apprehension and with gloom. Oh, restore me soon.
Psalm 6:2-3 (TLB)

The battle in my body occurred day and night. When I think things over, I realized how long my body was in the fight and how much pain it endured. My body had to fight as well during the fight of my life.

As I fought HIV behind closed doors, the battle in my body went forth day and night. The discomfort and pain I carried was obviously a serious issue and struggle for me. In the beginning, the shooting pains in my legs were hard to bare. The pains occurred in one leg at first. Eventually, the aches traveled in both of my legs.

On some days, regardless if I sat down or stood up, I endured the pain which arrived from having HIV and from being disobedient. The Word of God states, "Behold, to obey is better than sacrifice…," according to I Samuel 15:22. (KJV) The truth is, when you are disobedient, you will become the sacrifice, regardless of where the sacrifice will come from in your life.

One day as I was out shopping for a few groceries, the shooting pains evolved the more. They were now taking place in my back. With all of my might, I attempted not to cry because I was in the middle of a crowded grocery store. However, the pain was too much for me. I was hurting more than I thought I would. So, I quietly turned to a remote area in the store and released my tears. I did not care who saw them or what questions crossed their minds. The pain was awful. Although no one in the store realized why I was crying, I knew exactly why. All I wanted to do was disappear somewhere or just anywhere. Some days, I just wanted to die.

It seemed to me everyday went by slowly, except it included discomfort and pain. On certain days, my skin felt as if it wanted to tear itself apart. The pain was agonizing and my skin was on fire as if I was being tormented internally.

On some occasions, I found myself rushing to the mirror to see what was happening to me. Each time I approached the mirror, I found myself having anxiety attacks and emotional breakdowns. It seemed as if something on the inside wanted to come out from behind my skin. I believed the legions which form from HIV were trying to take root and surface.

At times, my skin looked like it was being tortured. Dark red spots formed on different parts of my body. They appeared and then disappeared. An assignment sent from hell was attacking my body and there was nothing I could do about it, but pray. I prayed all day and all night.

Then as I cried, I remember what my Pastor told me, "Whenever happens to you, I want you to speak to that condition and rebuke it!" "You have to release the Word of God over your life and tell yourself you are healed in Jesus Name!" This was the only thing that calmed my pain and kept me from having a nervous breakdown. I had to pray as if my life depended on it because it did.

On many occasions, I experienced intense headaches which were worse than migraines. The headaches I endured were almost humanly unbearable. I never fathomed headaches I encountered existed. Nothing made the pain depart from my human vessel.

When I attempted to take a couple of Advil P.M. tablets, nothing decreased or alleviated the deep, intense, reoccurring, throbbing pounding pressure. When I faced this demonic

The Fight of My Life!

attack, I quietly rested across my bed all day and definitely all night. I made sure I placed dark brown curtains over the other layer of curtains in my bedroom in order to survive the sharp, penetrating, sunlight shining through the foggy glass window in my bedroom.

I usually talked to the Lord in my heart and asked Him for His grace and mercy. I always went to Him like a child would go to His father, "Daddy, please have mercy on me." That was all I could do. That was the only strength I had at the time. It was too painful to move while I lay down.

Thus, I remained in a fetal position until the pain on that day and night slowly passed away. Yet, the HIV continued the same. It was still there like a thief in the night waiting for the next time to stand up against the Word of God which had been deposited in my Spirit. I was fighting for my life. Nevertheless, I was going to fight no matter what the test results stated.

The Fight of My Life!

The Second Test

The second test result was another blood test. I was HIV positive. I was holding on to the hand of the Lord.

*And we know
That all things
Work together for good
To them that love
God
To them who are
The called
According to his
Purpose.*
—**Romans 8:28 (KJV)**

Section 3

The Third Fight: Fighting For My Purpose

CHAPTER 14

Your Faith Must Stand Trial

LESSON 14

If you have ever been in a spiritual fight, there are two things you will have to face: your faith being stretched and your faith being on trial.

But without faith it is impossible to please him: for he that cometh to God must believe that he is, and that he is a rewarder of them that diligently seek him.
Hebrews 11:6 (KJV)

And without faith it is impossible to please God, because anyone who comes to him must believe that he exists and that he rewards those who earnestly seek him.
Hebrews 11:6 (NIV)

It's impossible to please God apart from faith. And why? Because anyone who wants to approach God must believe both that he exists and that he cares enough to respond to those who seek him.
Hebrews 11:6 (MSB)

You can never please God without faith, without depending on Him. Anyone who wants to come to God must believe that there is a God and that He rewards those who sincerely look for Him.
Hebrews 11:6 (TLB)

I discovered two components about faith during the fight of my life. I had to have faith to please God, I had to believe He would reward me for diligently seeking Him.

If you have ever been in a spiritual fight, there are two things you will have to face: your faith being stretched and your faith being on trial. That is where I was in 2013. My faith was being stretched every day and my faith was on trial for what seemed like a lifetime. However, in this courtroom, The Lord was the Judge and His Mighty Angels were the jury.

As it states in James 4:12, *"There is one lawgiver, who is able to save and to destroy: who art thou that judgest another?"* (KJV) Yet, the enemy which is referred as the 'accuser of the brethren' was lurking in the background of the matter and waited to hear what words would be released at the end of the trial. As a matter of fact, in the book of Revelation 12:9-10 the Word of The Lord reads it this way, *"And the great dragon was cast out, that old serpent, called the devil, and satan, which deceiveth the whole world: he was cast out into the earth, and his angels were cast out with him." "And I heard a loud voice saying in heaven, Now is come salvation, and strength, and the kingdom of our God, and the power of his Christ: for the accuser of our brethren is cast down, which accused them before our God day and night."*

The enemy desired to sift me as wheat, like the Word declares in Luke 22:31, *"And the Lord said, Simon, Simon, behold satan hath desired to have you, that he may sift you as wheat."* Regardless of what was happening, The Lord was my judge and my defense. In Psalm 94:22, the scripture illustrates that, *"But, the Lord is my defense; and my God is the rock of my refuge."*(KJV) By this, I knew Jesus was praying for me while my faith was standing trial.

There have been a few times in my life, I experienced what it was like having my faith tried in the fire. Thus, when I discovered I had HIV, this required another level of faith. My faith shifted to another dimension! My faith came alive! My faith had to be activated by the power of the Word of God. That is why the Word of God states in Hebrews 11:1 *"Now faith is the substance of things hoped for, the evidence of things not seen."*

My faith had an assignment to be stretched out – in order to pull down the healing in the area where I believed God. My faith had to be fully persuaded God would heal me, though I did not know what the final conclusion would be. I was hoping and believing, but still waiting on the manifestation.

There were specific moments when fear attempted to step in and say, *"Look at you, you have HIV!"* Then, I spoke back to it and released these words, *"I am healed in Jesus Mighty Name!"* That was the only way I arrested, captured and conquered the words the enemy tried to release concerning my faith.

Nonetheless, every day I woke up and left my house, I released a word of faith over my life. Faith became the supernatural medicine I used to destroy the HIV report which was surrounding the walls of my heart and my mind. That was the only way I survived.

Each day of the week, it appeared as if it was always another battle in front of me. Whether the battle was in my mind, in my heart or in my body, my faith was pushed where it had never gone before. Honestly, I know without a doubt,

The Fight of My Life!

if I would not have had the Lord to cry too and my *Pastor* to call on, I would not have made it through the struggle and my faith being on trial. Based on the Word in I John 5:4, it states this, *"For whatsoever is born of God overcometh the world: and this is the victory that overcometh the world, even our faith."* (KJV)

Faith was one of the most vital ingredients I chose while I waited to see what the end of the trial would be. This was the moment and the opportunity to see the God kind of faith on trial for the glory of the Lord.

All I could do was wait. However, while my faith was being examined, I waited in expectation of the Lord keeping me or the Lord healing me. Either way, I believed what the Lord could do and I believed what my *Pastor* told me, *"Is there anything too hard for the Lord?"*

Elizabeth Perkins

The Third Test

```
Powell-Perkins, ███ Elizabeth (MR # 074408273)

Results              ⚠ HIV-1/HIV-2 ROUTINE SCREENING (Accession M151266) (Order 147317299)
Entry Date
  8/20/2013
Component Results
  Component           Value         Flag    Low    High    Units    Status
  HIV-1/HIV-2         Positive      A                               Final
Result History
  HIV-1/HIV-2 ROUTINE SCREENING (Order #147317299) on 8/20/13 - Order Result History Report.
Lab Information
  Resulting Lab
  MISYS
Order Information
  Order Date                        Order Time
  Jul 15, 2013                      2:39 PM CDT
Result Information
  Result Date and Time              Status              Priority
  8/20/2013 8:12 AM                 Final result        Routine
Received Date/Time
  Received Date                     Received Time
  8/15/13                           7:48 AM
Result Notes
  ████████████████████████████████████████
  ████████████████████████████████████████
  ████████████████████████████████████████
Order Providers
  Authorizing Provider              Encounter Provider
  ████████████████                  ████████████████
Encounter
  View Encounter
Reviewed by List
  ████████████████
Order                ⚠ HIV-1/HIV-2 ROUTINE SCREENING [HIVRUS] (Order 147317299)
Administration Details
  No Administrations
  Recorded
Order Information
  Order Date/Time      Release Date/Time   Start Date/Time    End Date/Time
  7/15/2013 2:39 PM    None                7/15/2013          None
```

During the fight of my life, my blood test continued to test positive. I was still Believing God to heal me.

CHAPTER 15

The Delivery Room

LESSON 15

The delivery room is not just a room where you sit down and watch God. Rather, it is a spiritual place where you lay down for deliverance and God sits on you. That is what happened to me in the delivery room.

He shall call upon me, and I will answer him: I will be with him in trouble; I will deliver him, and honour him.
Psalm 91:15 (KJV)

He will call upon me, and I will answer him; I will be with him in trouble, I will deliver him and honor him.
Psalm 91:15 (NIV)

Call me and I'll answer, be at your side in bad times. I'll rescue you, then throw you a party.
Psalm 91:15 (MSB)

When he calls on me I will answer; I will be with him in trouble, and rescue him and honor him.
Psalm 91:15 (TLB)

Deliverance is freeing a person from a stronghold in the soulish realm. However, deliverance can also take place in the body for that person to be completely set free.

The delivery room is not just a room where you sit down and watch God. Rather, it is a spiritual place where you lay down for deliverance and God sits on you. That is what happened to me in the delivery room.

I needed healing from HIV and deliverance from the demonic attack attached to me. Therefore, my deliverance took place in– *the delivery room.* The delivery room was in the sanctuary at The Living Word Faith Center located in Missouri City, Texas. The delivery room was always available. However, the busiest days was on Sunday Morning at 10:30 a.m. and Sunday Evening at 5:00 p.m., during healing and deliverance service. This is where my surgical procedure took place.

I never had spiritual surgery like this before. I knew this one would be different. While in the delivery room, my Doctor was the Lord, but my Pastor was the surgeon. His specialty was healing and deliverance. His faith and his anointing was confirmed in the area of healing and deliverance in the United States as well as International.

His faith was tried in the fire on many occasions so he was prepared for this kind of fight. Actually, he always told us at church, *"It's another good day for the Lord and a bad day for the devil!"* He understood the spiritual fight and the process in the delivery room. I was in the delivery room several times before for other areas such as emotional healing, particularly dealing with the pains of my past. I cried out to the Lord and I was made free in this place. Thus, this healing could only happen in the delivery room. My deliverance would not be easy. Yet, the anointing of the Lord would be present. Soon thereafter, my surgery began.

The first thing which took place was my willingness to humble myself before the Lord and His presence. If I hoped to be healed, I had to be willing to fall at the feet of Jesus and be spiritually naked before Him. I needed His grace and mercy and His healing power to work in my life. I had to be a submitted vessel and willing participant while I was in the delivery room.

Secondly, I had to repent for the spiritual crime I committed against my body and for not following the warning the Lord sent my way. I willingly followed my flesh and now I had an emergency only the Lord could fix.

Forgiveness was also required. After my sexual crime was committed, anger and bitterness sat at the core of my heart. But, if I wanted the Lord to forgive me, I would have to render forgiveness to the person who committed this crime with me and against me.

Before every spiritual encounter I had with the Lord in the delivery room, I had to trust the Word of the Lord my Pastor gave me regarding my healing coming forth. He released healing words over my life although I could not see them immediately. The Word of the Lord states, *"Speak those things that be not as though they were."* Romans 4:17 (KVJ) This is what my Pastor did. Although the road seemed long and the trial attached to my healing was hard, I trusted what he said. He always reiterated to me, *"You have to believe God is a healer no matter what it looks like!"*

Another level of healing and deliverance which took place in the delivery room was the floor surgery. This is the where I had to be obedient to the voice of the Lord. With tears streaming down my face and my face on the floor, I yielded myself and my body to the presence and the power of the anointing of the Lord and allowed Him to sit on me.

During these moments where I knew supernatural healing was taking place, the presence of the Lord rested on my body as if I was in the surgery room with the presence of the Holy Spirit. I remembered the Lord would tell me, *"Just lay there and let me heal you."* I believe I was literally in His very presence of the Lord.

To be quite honest, when I was on the floor in the delivery room, I was not able to pick myself up from the floor. The presence of the Lord was so heavy upon me, I simply rested on the floor until several of the ministers were asked to pick me up until I sat up on my own. The Spirit of the Lord consumed me during those times. The Lord was healing my body. That is why I can truly testify that, *"The Lord is my healer!"*

CHAPTER 16
While You Are Waiting

LESSON

16

One of the hardest places in your life is when you are waiting for God to move, especially for a miracle. But, while you are waiting, you should know God is with you no matter how long you have to wait and no matter how much trouble you have to face.

When thou passest through the waters, I will be with thee; and through the rivers, they shall not overflow thee: when thou walkest through the fire, thou shalt not be burned: neither shall the flame kindle upon thee.
Isaiah 43:2 (KJV)

When you pass through the waters, I will be with you; and when you pass through the rivers, they will not sweep over you. When you walk through the fire, you will not be burned; the flames will not set you ablaze.
Isaiah 43:2 (NIV)

When you're in over your head, I'll be there with you. When you're in rough waters, you will not go down. When you're between a rock and a hard place, it won't be a dead end.
Isaiah 43:2 (MSB)

When you go through deep waters and great trouble, I will be with you. When you go through rivers of difficulty, you will not drown. When you walk through the fire of oppression, you will not be burned up – the flames will not consume you.
Isaiah 43:2 (TLB)

When you have to wait, you can wait on God or you can wait with God. Waiting with God means to wait on others until your waiting produces the miracle that you need.

While I was waiting, I believed the Lord for my healing, but I made room in my heart for more time of being in His presence, whether at church or at home. This was some of the most precious time I spent with the Lord in a while. From going to Church early to lay on the altar and stretching out on the floor in His presence at home, I was desperate for them both. I wanted to be in His presence more than anything else. His presence kept me alive and I was believing there was nothing too hard for the Lord.

During the waiting period, I remembered I had to come to a definite conclusion that I had to lean on the Lord for His strength and allow Him to carry me through this battle and fight. Waiting was one of the most challenges stages I encountered.

As my journey continued, I grasped three vital things while I was waiting. Although I was not in control of the final outcome of the fight I was experiencing, I was in control of the attitude I carried, how much I trusted the Lord and how much praise I rendered to the Lord while I waited for the manifestation of my healing.

In my heart I decided, I would trust God while I was waiting, work on my internal struggles and mindset until this battle was defeated and continue to praise Him until the fight was over. Even though the battle was not mine according to the Word of God, I still had to show up for this fight! I was in the fight on my life!

Therefore, I could not hide, while I was waiting. I could not allow the shame, embarrassment and the bad report to make me disappear from Church, the Kingdom and especially the Lord.

More than this, I had to overcome the mental and emotional pity party I invited into my heart and why I privately carried it around. I had to take full responsibility for my actions and my attitude. Truthfully, this was no one else's fault, but completely my own. Therefore, I could not walk around with a bad attitude or an emotional chip on my shoulder as if someone had wronged me.

Since I refused and did not to heed to the voice of the Lord when I received my warning – I had to not only wait with a good attitude, but I had to wait and love my neighbors and love my enemies also. That was one thing I vowed to the Lord I would do. I had to forgive fully, in order to be forgiven fully.

No matter how I felt mentally or physically, I would be faithful to the assignment the Lord gave me and illustrate His love towards every person that crossed my pathway. I refused to be judgmental regardless of what kind of issue someone else carried. I had to love my neighbor as myself.

Even so, this was one of the hardest places to be. I was hoping and praying the Lord would hear my cry and my prayers while I waiting.

The Fight of My Life!

The Fourth Test

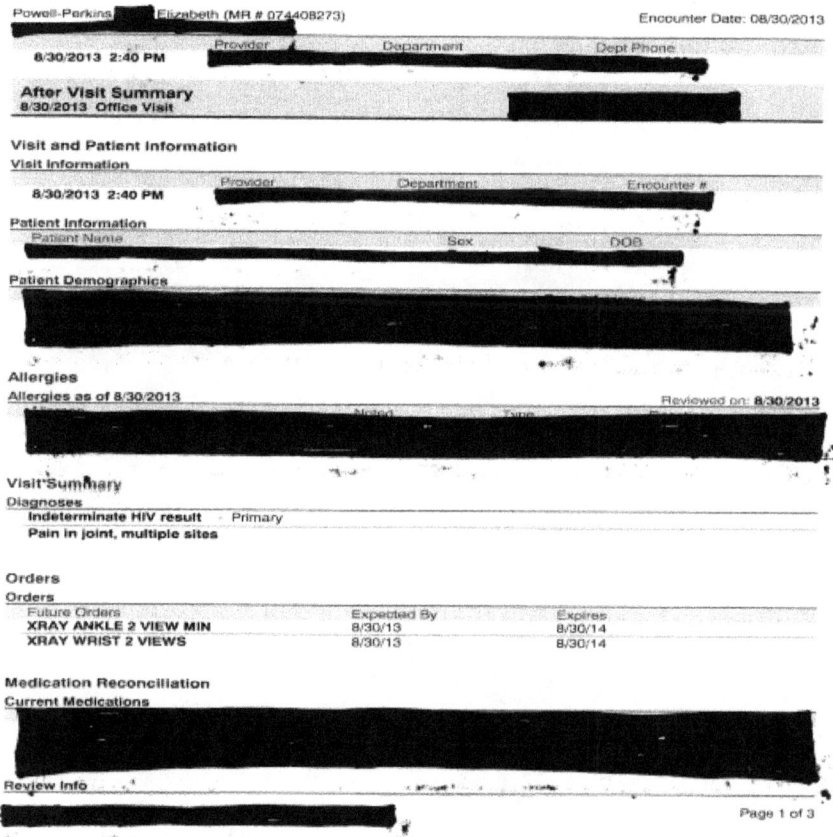

My journey of fighting took its course. Hence, my blood withdrawals continued as well. While I was waiting, I carried my pain with me as well.

CHAPTER 17

Somebody Needs Prayer

LESSON 17

A prayer is not just simple words released in the atmosphere. Rather, a prayer is a prophetic and strategic collection of anointed words with life discharged in the atmosphere and with an assignment attached to it for either healing or deliverance in order to set someone free.

And the prayer of faith shall save the sick, and the Lord shall raise him up; and if he have committed sins, they shall be forgiven him. Confess your faults one to another, and pray one for another, that ye may be healed. The effective fervent prayer of a righteous man availeth much.
James 5:15-16 (KJV)

And the prayer offered in faith will make the sick person well; the Lord will raise him up. If he has sinned, he will be forgiven. Therefore confess your sins to each other and pray for each other so that you may be healed. The prayer of a righteous man is powerful and effective.
James 5:15-16 (NIV)

Believing prayer will heal you, and Jesus will put you on your feet. And if you've sinned – you'll be forgiven – healed inside and out. Make this common practice. Confess your sins to each other and pray for each other so that you can live together whole and healed. The prayer of a person living right with God is something powerful to be reckoned with.
James 5:15-16 (MSB)

And their prayer, if offered in faith, will heal him, for the Lord will make him well; and if his sickness was caused by some sin, the Lord will forgive him. Admit your faults to one another and pray for each other so that you may be healed. The earnest prayer of a righteous man has great power and wonderful results.
James 5:15-16 (TLB)

I was fighting for my life and so were the prayers that were prayed over me. Words were spoken on the altar and on the threshing floor – which took place in the delivery room.

Somebody needs prayer. That was the situation in front of me while I worked at Obama Care Customer Service Center. I worked there briefly. Although I should have been walking in my destiny, I asked the Lord to use me while I was employed at this place. I worked at a call center before, but this one was quite different.

I always prayed for those at the center when I crossed their pathway, although some who worked there hated the mention of the name of Jesus. However, since I talked to people around the world – I soon knew I would be praying for others on the other side of the phone. Interestingly enough, I started pretty soon. Some of the prayers I prayed for the customers ranged from encouragement and of course, hoping to obtain insurance.

Not long after, the prayers became more intense. *The prayer requests I received from customers were prayers for HIV.* Initially, I was shocked. I was shocked because there were numerous calls which came through the lines concerning this disease. Some of them cried because they felt abandoned and rejected by people who they told.

Others cried and were extremely discouraged because they had no insurance and could not afford any insurance that was worth it. Moreover, I had many who shed tears and were greatly impacted because of their financial circumstances as well as being disowned by a mother, a father, a spouse or an entire family. Also, there were a few which were heavy burdened because they said they made a mistake during a time in their lives and they were now paying the price. The stories I heard never ended.

I always felt their pain on the other end of the phone. It was impossible not to understand what they were experiencing, since I had been diagnosed with HIV. My heart went out to them as I took their calls. Quite honestly, most of the calls I received came from men. Some were white. Some were black. Regardless of their color, they were all human. They had HIV!

Most importantly, they all desired prayer. One thing they had in common was– they all wanted to be either helped or healed! For sure, I knew they all needed to be encouraged. I could always hear the sound of sadness, pain and desperation on the other end of the phone.

Every time I heard a sound of desperation on the phone, I prayed for them, regardless of what might happen to me at the office. I did not care if I was fired or not! They were people and they mattered the most. Most importantly, I knew they mattered to God. The Lord still loved them, no matter what.

Even though I was in the fight of life. I had to put my fight on the shelf. I had to put my fight on hold while I fought for someone else. It was time for me to pray for another soul who was in need of healing or maybe even a miracle.

I had to visit my doctor and have my blood drawn while I worked at the center. However, between the presence of the Lord and the power of healing which took place in the delivery room at the Living Word Faith Center, somehow I knew I would be okay. My faith was stronger and my courage shifted to another place. My pity party left the core of my heart.

I was not sure if I would be healed, but I realized I was now in the hands of the Lord. His grace would be sufficient for me. Whatever verdict came my way, I had to minister to someone else. They deserved to know the Lord like I knew the Lord. I wanted them to understand there was grace, love, hope and healing available, if they only believed.

CHAPTER 18

Long Days And Long Nights

LESSON
18

When you are faced with sickness and disease in your body, often times you may experience long days and long nights. No matter what you are facing, the Lord will hold you up during the day and He will hold on to you at night.

Thou shalt not be afraid for the terror by night; nor for the arrow that flieth by day; Nor for the pestilence that walketh in darkness; nor for the destruction that wasteth at noonday. A thousand shall fall at thy side, and ten thousand at thy right hand; but it shall not come nigh thee.
Psalm 91: 5-7 (KJV)

You will not fear the terror of night, nor the arrow that flies by day, nor the pestilence that stalks in the darkness, nor the plague that destroys at midday. A thousand may fall at your side, but ten thousand at your right hand, but it will not come near you.
Psalm 91: 5-7 (NIV)

Fear nothing— not wild wolves in the night, not flying arrows in the day. Not disease that prowls through the darkness, not disaster that erupts at high noon. Even though others succumb all around, drop like flies right and left, no harm will even graze you.
Psalm 91: 5-7 (MSB)

Now you don't need to be afraid of the dark any more, nor fear the dangers of the day; nor dread the plagues of darkness, nor disasters in the morning. Though a thousand fall at my side, though ten thousand are dying around me, the evil will not touch me.
Psalm 91: 5-7 (TLB)

Thou shalt not be afraid for the terror by night; nor for the arrow that flieth by day; Nor for the pestilence that walketh in darkness; nor for the destruction that wasteth at noonday. A thousand shall fall at thy side, and ten thousand at thy right hand; but it shall not come nigh thee.
Psalm 91: 5-7 (KJV)

You will not fear the terror of night, nor the arrow that flies by day, nor the pestilence that stalks in the darkness, nor the plague that destroys at midday. A thousand may fall at your side, but ten thousand at your right hand, but it will not come near you.
Psalm 91: 5-7 (NIV)

Fear nothing– not wild wolves in the night, not flying arrows in the day. Not disease that prowls through the darkness, not disaster that erupts at high noon. Even though others succumb all around, drop like flies right and left, no harm will even graze you.
Psalm 91: 5-7 (MSB)

Now you don't need to be afraid of the dark any more, nor fear the dangers of the day; nor dread the plagues of darkness, nor disasters in the morning. Though a thousand fall at my side, though ten thousand are dying around me, the evil will not touch me.
Psalm 91: 5-7 (TLB)

LESSON

18

When you are faced with sickness and disease in your body, often times you may experience long days and long nights. No matter what you are facing, the Lord will hold you up during the day and He will hold on to you at night.

I remember the long days and long nights I endured while I was fighting for my life. I dealt with depression, darkness, pain and fear. Still, I knew the Lord was fighting for me behind the scenes – in order to set me free.

My days and my nights were long. During this period, the warfare and the fight was present. I was battling extreme migraine headaches. By this time, the headaches intensified. Some days I carried the headaches with me to work and fought with them at night. The fight of my life was in full progress, but I was trusting God to fight for me.

One morning, I was on my way to work and my body was aching allover. I wanted to work Friday to close off the week. As soon I arrived, I was sick. After a manager saw me, she gave me permission to go home. As a result, I stayed there shortly, turned around and left. I didn't recognize what came upon me, but I thought it was possibly the flu. However, battling the flu and the HIV was more than I wanted to fight together.

It was going around the center at the time. Yet, it hit my immune system and my body all at once. I remember when I came home, threw up and lay on my bathroom floor. That was the only strength I had. I was so sick I could barely move.

I sure couldn't eat anything, at least for a couple of days. One of those days, the fever from the flu took over. My fever was about 102 degrees. I called on the name of Jesus. I drove myself to the emergency room to see if something could be done for me. After I waited for an hour, the doctor told me there was nothing they could do, except prescribe Tylenol for the fever and rest in bed for three to four days. So, I followed their instructions and went back home and rested. It took about a week to fully recover. Eventually, my strength returned enough and I went back to work.

The next battle I fought was cold sweats at night and body aches. The shakes took over my body reminded me of how I saw someone's body move from being on drugs – when they were trying to detox.

Most of the days and nights when I battled flu like systems and cold sweats at night, there was nothing I could do, except for cry out and call on the name of Jesus. After I called out to Him, I rested until He strengthened my body to get back up again.

By this time, my assignment in the call center was coming to an end, I realized the Lord did something while I was there. The opportunity He gave me to pray for the sick, the discouraged, the brokenhearted and especially for those who called on the phone with HIV. Every call was worth every minute of my time. Every soul mattered. When my last day came, I remembered the people I met over the phone who received prayer. One thing I will never forget are those who felt as if everything was over in their lives because they had HIV. Before I ended a call, I always reminded them they would 'live and not die!' I prayed for as many people as I could! They were many.

I thought to myself, "What was the best thing that happened to me while I was there?" It was because somebody needed prayer. Moreover, God answered their prayers through someone just like them. I was carrying what they were carrying. I understood their story.

I understood their pain. That is what mattered to me the most. I wanted them to know that after I prayed for them, The Lord would fight the battle for them as well. I felt compelled to pray for them. Their faith was on trial and so was mine. I refused to give up on them. They needed encouragement, faith and healing just like I did. I wanted to pray for them and I wanted to fight for their lives!

Elizabeth Perkins

The Fifth Test Result

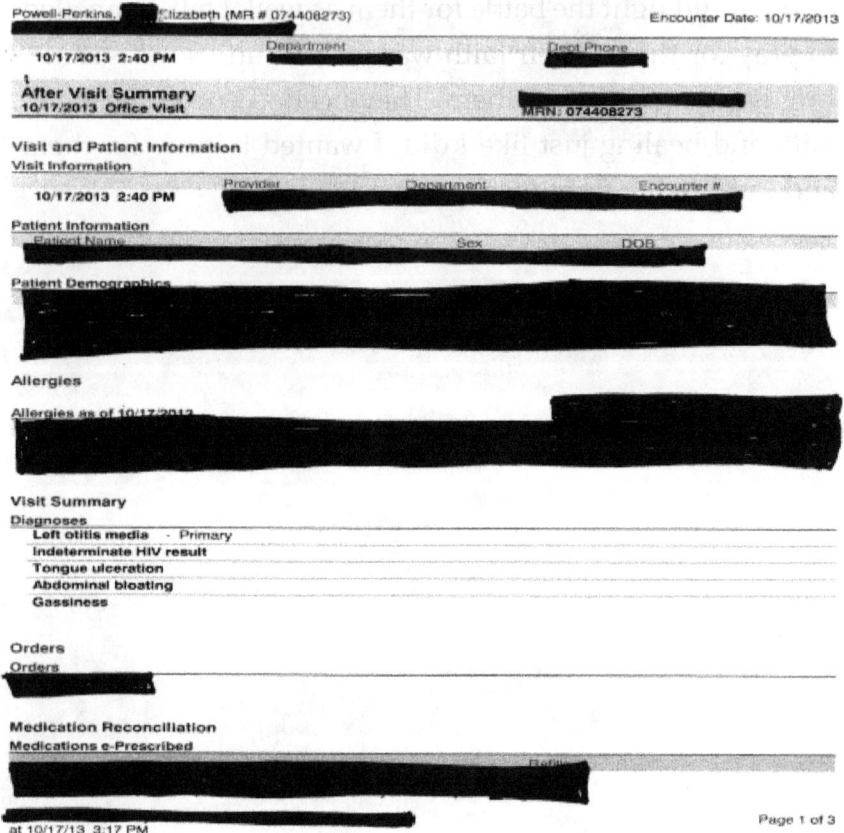

The test was still positive. The battle was not over. I had to fight for my life.

I shall not die,
But live,
And declare
The works of
The Lord.
—Psalm 188:117 (KJV)

Section 4

The Fourth Fight: Fighting For My Healing

CHAPTER 19

You Will Live And Not Die

LESSON

19

Often times, you never think about your life until you are faced with the possibility of death or someone else dying close to you. That is when you finally realize it is only God who has kept the death angel away and made death obey.

The Fight of My Life!

I shall not die, but live, and declare the works of the Lord. The Lord hath chastened me sore: but he hath not given me over unto death.
Psalm 118:17-18 (KJV)

I will not die but live, and will proclaim what the Lord has done. The Lord has chastened me severely, but he has not given me over to death.
Psalm 118:17-18 (NIV)

I did not die! I lived! And now, I am telling the world what God did. God tested me, he pushed me hard, but he didn't hand me over to Death.
Psalm 118:17-18 (MSB)

I shall not die, but live to tell of all his deeds. The Lord has punished me, but not handed me over to Death.
Psalm 118:17-18 (TLB)

There were moments when I wanted to die, but I needed to live. While I was fighting and dealing with battles on every side, I always remembered these words, "You will live and not die!" These were the prophetic words that were spoken over my life.

You will live and not die! Those were the words my Pastor spoke over my life when I was in the fight of my life. The fight was real, but the battle was the Lord's. The enemy was trying to kill, steal and destroy my life and my faith in the Lord.

I had to believe the Lord for my healing as well as my deliverance, but I couldn't do it alone. In order for that to take place, I remained steadfast in my journey and my time in the delivery room at both church services. Both were needed and both were available. Truthfully, I never missed healing and deliverance service. The Word of God was always true, the atmosphere was anointed and the Spirit of the Lord was always present to meet anyone there who was serious about deliverance in their lives.

Although, I had not told a soul because of the embarrassment and shame I carried, I had to be willing to lay on the altar and release myself at the feet of Jesus in the delivery room. Every time I had a hard week and I wanted to give up the fight, my Pastor always reminded me of the scripture. *You will live and not die and declare the works of the Lord!* I thought to myself, *"How could I?"* He reiterated to me, *"You are going to have to believe!" "You still have purpose and destiny over your life!"*

When I received the report from the doctor, I definitely thought I would not live long. My body sent me signals all of the time which represented pain. Yet, the healing and deliverance service always reminded me about the power of prayer and the power of the presence of the Lord!

That is what kept me while I was fighting between two opinions of, *"Will I live? Or Will I die?"* Therefore, the Word I received during healing and deliverance service allowed me to understand the power of healing and the power of the presence of the Lord. After I calmed the battle in my mind, I spoke the words over my life every day – 'I would live and not die!' That was one way I fought the good fight of faith and the fight of my life! It was hard, but it was necessary for me to fight this fight with the Word and the Worship!

The Fight of My Life!

The Six Test Result

```
Powell-Perkins, ▮▮▮ Elizabeth (MR # 074408273)          Encounter Date: 01/10/2014
                                Department              Dept Phone
1/10/2014  3:00 PM
After Visit Summary
1/10/2014  Office Visit                                 MRN: 074408273

Visit and Patient Information
Visit Information
                      Provider       Department         Encounter #
1/10/2014  3:00 PM
Patient Information
    Patient Name                        Sex             DOB
Patient Demographics


Allergies
Allergies as of 1/10/2014                        Fully Assessed On: 1/10/20▮


Visit Summary
Diagnoses
    Indeterminate HIV result   - Primary
    Bone pain
    Sinus congestion

Orders
Orders

    Future Orders               Expected By      Expires
                                1/13/14          1/31/14

Medication Reconciliation
Medications NOT e-Prescribed
                                Dosage
```

    The sixth test result represented another positive blood test. I was still believing God for a miracle.

CHAPTER 20

I Know It Was The Blood

LESSON

20

The Lord is a God of miracles as well as numbers. He is a strategic God. He is a God of order, even when it comes to how many days it takes for a miracle to take place in your life. His miracles are never late, but always on time.

And, behold, there was a woman which had a spirit of infirmity eighteen years, and was bowed together, and could in no wise lift up herself. And, when Jesus saw her, he called her to him, and said unto her, Woman thou art loosed from thine infirmity.
Luke 13:11-12 (KJV)

And a woman was there who had been crippled by a spirit for eighteen years. She was bent over and could not straighten up at all. When Jesus saw her, he called her forward and said to her,
Woman, you are set free from your infirmity.
Luke 13:11-12 (NIV)

There was a woman present, so twisted and bent over with arthritis that she couldn't even look up. She had been afflicted with this for eighteen years. When Jesus saw her, he called her over. Woman, you're free.
Luke 13:11-12 (MSB)

He saw a seriously handicapped woman who had been bent double for eighteen years and was unable to straighten herself. Calling her over to him Jesus said, Woman you are healed of your sickness.
Luke 13:11-12 (TLB)

3 is the number for wholeness and completion. 8 is the number of new beginnings and resurrection. God is a God of numbers, but He is also a God of miracles. God gave me another miracle when the blood from my body came streaming down.

38days. This was the amount of time I bled. In John 5:5-6, the Bible demonstrates, *"And a certain man was there, which had an infirmity thirty and eight years. When Jesus saw him lie, and knew that he had been now a long time in that case, He saith unto him, Wilt thou be made whole?"* (KJV)

What was happening inside my body? I could not understand what triggered this? Normally, my menstrual cycle lasted for five days. This time it was different. It all started during a leadership conference I was attending in San Antonio, Texas. The bleeding was tremendously heavy. While the meeting was in full swing, I recognized I had to dismiss myself and go the bathroom. Honestly, I rushed to get there. The blood was streaming down more than I imagined. My strength seemed somewhat depleted. I was quietly panicking.

When I returned to Houston, I made an appointment with another doctor. It was urgent as far as I was concerned. Immediately, the doctor entered the office and gave me instructions to place my body on the medical table. For a moment, I was attempting to ask her to provide me with medication to stop the bleeding because of the heaviness. As I sat there, I heard the Lord say to me, *"Don't you trust me?"* I responded quickly, *"Yes. Lord. I do."*

So, without a struggle or a reason of doubt, I explained to the doctor I decided not to be examined. I soon left and went home. As I drove, tears begin to fall. My gratefulness tilted to another level that the Lord spoke to me. Regardless of how it looked, I was determined to trust the Lord more than ever.

While I stayed on this journey of trusting the Lord with this fight, I remembered saying to myself this scripture, *"Is not God the God of all flesh?"* My body was in need of healing and cleansing. As a result, the blood continued to flow. The blood went from mere small deposits to the size of quarters. I didn't know what was happening in my body!

During this time period, I was not able to do much activity on a lot of days because I was bleeding so heavy most of the time. I never bled this much before. Some days, I felt faint because the amount of blood being released from my body. My menstrual cycle went from 5 days to 38 days. *The blood which came streaming down occurred for 38 days without ceasing. It was pouring out like a flood.* What was happening in my vessel of clay? What could this possibly be?

Yet, I told the Lord I would trust Him and hold on to what I was believing. I was depending on the Lord for a miracle. Doing so, I made sure I always reminded the Lord of my vow I made to Him. If you heal me Lord, I will tell the world what you did!

At the end of the **38 days**, I Biblically understood and prophetically concluded the number – *three means divine completeness, wholeness and perfection. The number eight means resurrection and a new beginning.* Everything which took place in my body, happened for a reason. However, the one thing I didn't know was, would there be a miracle after the blood came streaming down?

The Fight of My Life!

The Seventh Test Result

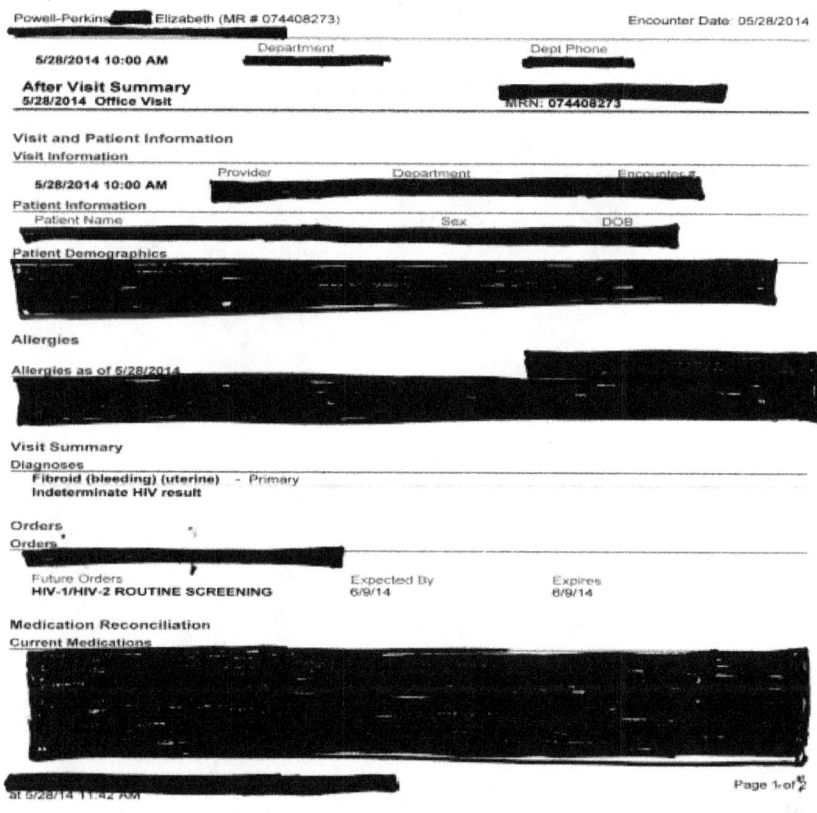

The seventh test result was now complete. I was still waiting on the verdict. Would I be healed?

CHAPTER 21

Sunday Morning Power Prayer

LESSON

21

Prayer is decreeing and declaring the power of the Word of God, mixing it with faith, delivering it into the atmosphere of heaven and the throne room of God while giving God total thanksgiving and adoration with all of your heart, soul, mind and will.

Be careful for nothing; but in everything by prayer and supplication with thanksgiving let your requests be made known unto God.
Philippians 4:6 (KJV)

Do not be anxious about anything, but in everything, by prayer and petition with thanksgiving, present your requests to God.
Philippians 4:6 (NIV)

Don't fret or worry. Instead of worrying, pray. Let petitions and praises shape your worries into prayers, letting God know your concerns.
Philippians 4:6 (MSB)

Don't worry about anything; instead, pray about everything; tell God your needs and don't forget to thank Him for His answers.
Philippians 4:6 (TLB)

Prayer is not just words you say, but it is words you believe with all of your heart, soul, mind and will. Thus, when you pray, you have to pray as if the healing is already here and the miracle is already done.

Nothing happens without prayer. That is why I believe one of the greatest gifts a person can have is the ability to prayer for someone else. Another strength a person can have is to be able to pray as well as touch and agree with another person while he or she stands believing God to bring a miracle to pass.

With that being said, I know for sure one of the most honorable callings to have is to be an intercessor. ***An Intercessor is one who intercedes on behalf of someone's life or problem, regardless of what that maybe.***

As such, the Lord has allowed me to intercede on behalf of others on many occasions, whether it was at the altar during a ministry meeting or at church service. On Sunday Mornings, there were several Sundays when I was allowed to lead prayer at church. Specifically, I recall one Sunday Morning when I asked my Pastor if he still desired for me to lead Sunday Morning Prayer. He responded, *"Of course."*

I was surprised, but I should not have been taken off guard since he had always been a Pastor of Faith. So he stated to me, *"Why wouldn't I want you to pray?"* I responded, *"I thought it would be better for someone else to pray because of my condition."* He looked at me and said plainly, *"I want you to pray this morning."*

As far as I was concerned, I always loved prayer. But, this time prayer felt different. It seemed to me when I prayed, something was occurring in the atmosphere. I felt heaven move. I sensed the presence of the Lord in the delivery room himself.

I could not quite explain it. It was not something tangible you could feel in the natural. It was something you had to touch in the spirit realm. I called it a supernatural takeover. I entered another dimension like the woman with the issue of blood!

I wanted to have a face to face encounter with the Lord like she did. I had my blood drawn over and over again and it was still contaminated with a disease. I not only wanted to be healed, but I desired to be made whole. I wanted to tell the Lord the entire story of my life of how I became like I was! On that morning, I wanted to touch the hem of His garment!

One thing I knew for sure, the Spirit of God was in the delivery room and deliverance was taking place! I wasn't sure if it was for me. I was interceding for those in the sanctuary. Yet, every time I prayed, I felt the presence of the Lord even stronger. His presence was in the room. He was moving. I felt His glory in the delivery room. It was so strong during *Sunday Morning Power Prayer!*

After Sunday Morning Power Prayer went forth, I went back to my seat as usual. However, this time it was not as usual. Someone who was sitting behind me made a statement to me. She released the words, *"God is going to give you a miracle!"* I don't remember what I told her exactly. I do remember giving the Lord praise for such a mighty time in prayer that morning. The presence of the Lord was in the service and I felt something happen!

To be honest, I was so happy to feel the presence, the power and the praise in the room going forth, my mind was removed from even thinking about HIV. It never crossed my mind that morning. So, when I received those words, I was excited to know the Lord was moving!

By this time, I cast my concerns and my cares about the HIV fully on the Lord. Although I had to show up for the fight, the battle was not mine any longer, but it was the Lord's! From that moment, I couldn't handle worrying anymore!

After I prayed, I gave everything to Him. I made up my mind. I was fully persuaded I had to do His will, whether He healed me or not! I had to continue to give Him praise for who He was, whether I was healed or not! He deserved the praise because He was still God!

CHAPTER 22
When Praises Go Up

LESSON

22

A Praise is when you release a forcible prophetic sound birthed from the chambers of the heart and from the bottom of a yielded soul. It is then released through the mouth to the atmosphere of heaven and finally into the throne room of God.

Be careful for nothing; but in everything by prayer and supplication with thanksgiving let your requests be made known unto God.
Philippians 4:6 (KJV)

Do not be anxious about anything, but in everything, by prayer and petition with thanksgiving, present your requests to God.
Philippians 4:6 (NIV)

Don't fret or worry. Instead of worrying, pray. Let petitions and praises shape your worries into prayers, letting God know your concerns.
Philippians 4:6 (MSB)

Don't worry about anything; instead, pray about everything; tell God your needs and don't forget to thank Him for His answers.
Philippians 4:6 (TLB)

Praise is when words are released from the human mouth to a heavenly God. Thus, praise is the ultimate celebration of decreeing and declaring the glory of God from earth to heaven.

Have you ever been in a grave situation when your back was against the wall and you were fighting for your life? What did you do? Did you go into a pity party? Or did you break out into a praise? Did you give the Lord some worship even though you did not know what the outcome of your fight would be?

Well, I remember when I was facing the fight of my life. All I had was a praise! Do you know the power that is in a *praise*? Let me explain it this way. The Word of God says, *"I will sing to the Lord as long as I live; I will sing praise to my God while I have my being!"* Psalm 104:33 (KJV) It was praise and worship the Lord used to pull me out of some of the hardest times when I was feeling down and completely discouraged.

There were moments while I was sitting in church service or during a revival and the spirit of heaviness or depression would sit on me. My countenance was dark and my spiritual strength was at an all-time low. I had to quickly find a scripture in the Word to pull down those strongholds. One specific scripture I often used was found in 2 Corinthians 10: 4-5. This Word says, *"For the weapons of our warfare are not carnal, but mighty through God to the pulling down of strongholds; casting down imaginations…and bringing into captivity every thought to the obedience of Christ!"* Another scripture I depended on when the enemy was fighting my mind was, *"The joy of the Lord is my strength!"* Nehemiah 8:10 (KJV) ***The root word for 'joy' means to make glad or rejoice! 'Strength' means to be in a place of safety, a refuge, to make strong, or to strengthen.*** I recognized that if I allowed the enemy to take the joy or the strength that I had remaining, my fight would grow worse if I did not fight back!

Have you ever had a grew worse moment? I felt like I was experiencing a grew worse moment, for sure! The more I prayed and the more I praised, the enemy tried to remind me that I wasn't going to be healed! Nonetheless, I always reminded the enemy that he was a liar! I had to remind the enemy daily the Word of God said, *I shall not die, but live and declare the works of the LORD!"* Psalm 118:17 *(KJV)*

Since, I was fighting for my life, I knew I had to continue to deposit scriptures in my mind and in my spirit that would give me spiritual strength during this battle of spiritual warfare. I was still believing the Lord to heal me. I was still standing on His Word! As such, I had to use my praise and worship to defeat the enemy I could not see! Since the Lord drew me from the darkness of the enemy's camp to His marvelous light, I have always found myself giving the Lord praise as well as worship! Moreover, while I was writing, this is the definition the Lord gave me for praise. ***A praise is when you release a forcible prophetic sound birthed from the chambers of the heart and from the bottom of a yielded soul. It is then released through the mouth to the atmosphere of heaven and finally into the throne room of God!*** That is why I know for sure, there is power in praise! Without a doubt, the Word of God says, *"Let everything that hath breath praise the Lord!"* Psalm 150:6 (KJV) Praise was the very ingredient I needed to lift my spirit and keep my mind out of the pit! The Bible says in Psalm 103:1-22, *"Bless the Lord O my soul, and all that* is within me, bless his holy name!" Bless the Lord, O my soul, and forget not all of his benefits…who redeems your life from the pit…so that your youth is renewed like the eagles." (KJV) Another book of Psalm 95:6 reads, "Oh come, let us worship and bow down; let us kneel before the Lord, our Maker!" (KJV)

That is why I believe one of the greatest weapons I used to encourage myself was my praise and my worship! I rendered the Lord a praise every morning, noon and night. Every time I gave the Lord praise I could feel His presence! During church services I always praised the Lord without any reservation. I danced before Him with all of my might! *I entered His gates with thanksgiving, and his courts with praise! Give thanks to him; bless his name!* Psalm 100:4 (KJV) Regardless of how I felt, I had to fight for my praise because the Lord had kept me thus far. Sometimes, my body did not always feel good. Truthfully, there were some days that I did not feel well. On certain days, my body felt like it had the flu, but just times ten! Other times, my body just felt bad or exhausted.

Nevertheless, I had no right to be angry at the Lord when He was the very person that allowed me to be alive! In my mind, whether my praise was high or low, I always found a praise in my heart and a praise on my lips. As far as I was concerned, my body was under attack, but my mouth was still free! Every time a praise went up into the atmosphere of heaven and to the throne room of the LORD, I believe my healing came down. But, I still had to believe the LORD would give me a miracle!

CHAPTER 23

Do You Believe In Miracles?

LESSON

23

A miracle is not natural, but it is supernatural. God releases the supernatural manifestation of healing and deliverance from the heavenly realm to the natural realm. Therefore, it takes God to make a miracle come to pass. However, it takes you to believe God can do it and for death to be swallowed up in victory.

Death is swallowed up in victory! O death, where is thy sting? O grave, where is thy victory?
I Corinthians 15:54 – 55 (KJV)

Death has been swallowed up in victory! Where, O death, is your victory? Where, O death, is your sting?
I Corinthians 15: 54 – 55 (NIV)

Death swallowed by triumphant Life! Who got the last word, oh Death? Oh, Death, who's afraid of you now?
I Corinthians 15: 54 – 55 (MSB)

When this happens, then at last this scripture will come true – Death is swallowed up in victory! O, death, where then your victory? Where then your sting?
I Corinthians 15: 54 – 55 (TLB)

A miracle is not what you see first, but, it is what you believe without being able to see. Hence, when you are in need of a miracle, you will be required to stretch your faith and walk by faith even if you cannot see.

A miracle is not natural, but it is supernatural. God releases the supernatural manifestation of healing and deliverance from the heavenly realm to the natural realm. Therefore, it takes God to make a miracle come to pass. However, it takes you to believe God can do it and for death to be swallowed up in victory.

There I was in 2013. I had HIV. I was in need of a supernatural miracle by the Lord. I could have lived as I was, but I hated living with this condition. The pain I experienced, the discomfort I endured and the days and nights I was sick, I wanted to be healed.

It was too much for me to carry physically, emotionally, psychologically and mentally. Every area of my life was impacted. I never felt clean. I always found myself taking bath after bath hoping I could wipe the HIV away. Yet, I knew it was not going anywhere without a miracle being released from heaven.

At the time, I believed in miracles for other people, but my faith had not been tried in the fire for a miracle for myself. Although the Word of God states in Jeremiah 32:27, *"Is there anything too hard for the Lord?"* Thus, I knew in my heart this definitely would be hard for me – but not for the Lord.

I prayed the Lord would hear my cry and render a miracle in my life. If He healed me, I would repay Him by releasing my testimony to the world, no matter what anyone said or thought of me. He was the potter and I was the clay.

His healing was worth more than anyone else's opinion or words. Whose opinion would I believe? Whose opinion mattered the most? What it be the Lord's or would it be someone else's? I only wanted to believe the report of the Lord! Nothing else mattered.

I remember always believing miracles for other people, but I never recognized the power of a miracle until it concerned my own life. One day my miracle came my way.

I returned to my doctor the week prior to having my blood drawn. It was time to see what the report read. I adjusted my mind, my thoughts and my emotions, so I could put them in their proper place since I was use to going to the doctor on a regular basis by now.

I assumed this visit would be like the others. I also thought the report concerning the HIV would be the same too. However, when my doctor walked in the room, she pulled up the test results from the computer while I sat in the chair in the office.

At first she stared at the computer screen. Then, all of a sudden, she stated to me, *"Come over here!"* So, I instantly looked right back at her and she said it again, *"Come over here!"* She told me to look at the screen. Then, she said, *"Read It!"*

As I read the test results from the report, I said to her, *"The test results from the HIV are negative!"* Then, she stated to me, *"They can't find anything in your blood!"*

I cried intensely as I read the doctor's report! Immediately, tears of joy from my heart and soul came forth as if they waited to hear those words! I fell on my knees right there in the office, kneeled down on the floor and I gave the Lord praise! I praise Him not only because He healed me – but because He heard my cry!

I was healed! No matter what anyone concluded concerning this matter, the Lord showed up and performed the miracle I was waiting for while I was fighting for my life! He healed me of this condition I carried in my blood stream! He healed me from HIV!

The tears of joy from believing the Lord what seemed like an eternity finally manifested itself from the spiritual to the natural. I was healed supernaturally and the Lord set me free! Now, I could go and spread the good news the Lord, Jesus was still a healer!

Most importantly, I could tell them – there is nothing too hard for the Lord, if you only believe!

Elizabeth Perkins

The Eight Test Result

```
Powell-Perkins,     Elizabeth (MR # 074408273)

Results              HIV-1/HIV-2 ROUTINE SCREENING (Accession W557602) (Order 170738472)
Entry Date
  6/11/2014
Component Results
  Component        Value       Flag    Range    Units    Status
  HIV-1/HIV-2      Negative            NEG               Final
  Comment
    Discrepancy from previous results noted, please repeat for confirmation
Result History
  HIV-1/HIV-2 ROUTINE SCREENING (Order #170738472) on 6/11/14 - Order Result History Report
Lab Information
  Resulting Lab
    MISYS
Order Information
  Order Date                             Order Time
  Jun 11, 2014                           11:19 AM CDT
Result Information
  Result Date and Time    Status            Priority
  6/11/2014 5:53 PM       Final result      Routine
Received Date/Time
  Received Date                          Received Time
  6/11/14                                11:21 AM
Order Providers
  Authorizing Provider                   Encounter Provider

Encounter
  View Encounter

Order                HIV-1/HIV-2 ROUTINE SCREENING [HIVRUS] (Order 170738472)
Administration Details
  No Administrations
  Recorded
Order Information
  Order Date/Time     Release Date/Time    Start Date/Time     End Date/Time
  5/28/2014 1:12 PM   6/11/2014 11:19 AM   6/11/2014           None
Order Details
  Frequency           Duration             Priority            Order Class
  None                None                 Routine             Normal
Quantity
  Ordering Quantity
  1
Original Order
  Ordered On                             Ordered By
  Wed May 28, 2014 1:12 PM
Associated Diagnoses
  Indeterminate HIV result
```

The eighth test result...The miracle I desired and beleived manifested itself.

CHAPTER 24

The Fight Of My Life

LESSON

24

There are a few fights you may have to fight. However, one of your greatest fights will be the fight for your life. You will fight the hardest. But, the Lord will win the battle, if you truly believe.

Wherefore take into you, the whole armor of God, that he may be able to withstand in the evilday, and having done all to stand.
Ephesians 6:13 (KJV)

Therefore, put on the full armor of God, so that when the day of evil comes, you may be able to stand your ground, and after you have done everything, to stand.
Ephesians 6: 13 (NIV)

Be prepared. You are up against far more than you can handle on your own. Take all the help you can get, every weapon God has issued, so that when it's all over you will still be shouting on your feet.
Ephesians 6:13 (MSG)

So use every piece of God's armor to resist the enemy whenever he attacks, and when it is all over, you will still be standing up.
Ephesians 6:13 (TLB)

While I was fighting for my life on my knees, Jesus was standing in the throne room fighting for me.

Even though ***The Fight Of My Life*** is over, I realized another fight had only just begun. The story of what happened to me, how I was healed from HIV supernaturally by the LORD and how my healing and deliverance took place in the delivery room at *The Living Word Faith Center in Missouri City, Texas* had to be told around the world!I made a vow to the Lord. I promised Him. That promise had to be kept. Moreover, I made a declaration to turn my pain into my purpose.

This was not only another testimony, but this journey of truth, trials, trust and triumph was also because my Pastor prayed me through the darkest days, times and moments of my life and went into battle face to face with the enemy to defeat a sickness which almost stole my destiny.

With all of my heart, I celebrate The Lord Jesus Christ and give Him all the glory for His grace and mercy and healing anointing which was evident in the delivery room where His presence sat on me every Sunday morning and Sunday evening during healing and deliverance service.

Although I had the fight of my life with HIV, there were other small battles which confronted me during the battle. One major fight was for my mind. This was the place where I had the hardest struggle. My mind was constantly in spiritual warfare.

No day passed by where I was not fighting with the enemy. From days of depression and despair to a few rays of hope, I faced them all. I was in constant battle to keep my mind from falling into a dark abyss. It was a continuous fight. This was one of the greatest battles of my life.

Another fight I endured was my faith. It appeared as if everything was on trial, particularly my faith. Not knowing what was going to happen to me was completely terrifying. However, believing the Lord would heal me was another dimension of faith.

With that being said, I did not think I would have found the courage to write this story because it was not a story full of beautiful rose petals, but sharp and painful thorns which represented pain, discomfort and longsuffering possibly with no joyful ending.

Nevertheless, I made a vow to the Lord that if He healed me, I would tell the world what He did. I would put proof on paper for anyone to read and conclude Jesus is a healer! He is still Lord! For that reason, He deserved the glory. He deserved all the praise.

As a result of telling this story, line by line and precept by precept; I hope to encourage and uplift those who are fighting for their lives and waging war against HIV or any disease known to mankind. I aim to remind them the Bible says in 2 Chronicles 20:15, *"For the battle is not yours, but God's."*(KJV) Though the battle ultimately belongs to God, you still have to show up for the fight. That is exactly what I did! I had to endure – the fight of my life!

As such, I desire to reiterate to some and to sound the alarm to others that there is still a fight in the supernatural for their lives! Moreover, there is also a place called the delivery room where the Lord is still alive and healing and deliverance takes place!

It is in this place where God will demonstrate to you all things are possible if you have the faith even the size of a mustard seed! Though you still have to show up for the fight of your life - there is one thing that you need to remember.

The LORD will always win the battle, but you must always believe, especially if you had to fight the greatest battle like this one...

The Fight Of My Life

Elizabeth Perkins

The Final Test

Powell-Perkins, ▮ Elizabeth (MR # 074408273)

Results	HIV-1/HIV-2 ROUTINE SCREENING (Accession M1103263) (Order 200970345)				
Entry Date					
7/27/2015					
Component Results					
Component	Value	Flag	Ref Range	Units	Status
HIV-1/HIV-2	Negative		NEG		Final
Result History					
HIV-1/HIV-2 ROUTINE SCREENING (Order #200970345) on 7/27/15 - Order Result History Report					
Lab Information					
Resulting Lab					
MISYS					
Order Information					
Order Date		Order Time			
Jul 27, 2015		12:29 PM CDT			
Result Information					
Result Date and Time	Status	Priority			
7/27/2015 5:57 PM	Final result	Routine			
Received Date/Time					
Received Date		Received Time			
7/27/15		12:54 PM			
Result Notes					

Order Providers

Encounter
View Encounter

Reviewed by List

Order	HIV-1/HIV-2 ROUTINE SCREENING [HIVRUS] (Order 200970345)
Patient Name	

Administration Details
No Administrations Recorded

Order Information
Order Date/Time   Release Date/Time   Start Date/Time   End Date/Time

The final test result....The final test result was the conclusion of the matter. The Lord healed me.

*And they
Overcame him
By the
Blood of the lamb
And by the word
Of their testimony.*
—Revelation 12:18 (KJV)

About The Book

This book is like no other. **Elizabeth Perkins,** *Prophetess, Pastor, Teacher, Author* and *Poet* takes you on an authentic journey of what happened when she was diagnosed with HIV. She comes clean about how her disobedience and falling into sin almost cost her everything. She carried the shame she had only heard others talk about when it came to being infected with HIV.

There she was. She was without question and totally unequivocally in the fight of her life. She knew this fight was real. This fight was serious. This was definitely her fault. However, there was one thing she came to grips with immediately. She could not win this fight without the LORD.

Yet, she had to go to the Lord with complete honesty, sincerity, desperation and repentance. He was her only hope. As the tears from her eyes rolled slowly down her face after the conclusion of the doctor's report, she recognized she would carry this condition forever, unless the LORD healed her. She was in need of a miracle just like the woman with the issue of blood. Her blood was contaminated.

As she battled this sickness and condition underneath the radar of her everyday life along with days of discouragement and feeling unclean, she talks about the truth, test, trials and tribulations she experienced along this dark road.

While she was believing the Lord for her healing, she found the courage and the faith to take her eyes off her condition and begin to pray for others who were carrying the disease and other illnesses. After she experienced many days and many nights of battling this sickness, bled for thirty eight days straight and endured nine long months of carrying HIV, God gave her the miracle of her life. God healed her. It was not man. It was not the doctor. It was God. He healed her from HIV.

In the end of this journey and hard lessons of life, Prophetess Elizabeth Perkins discovered there is nothing too hard for the Lord. There is nothing too hard for anyone who has an illness or a condition of any kind, if you only believe in miracles as she did in this book…

The Fight Of My Life

Books By Prophetess Elizabeth Perkins

EXCESS BAGGAGE
How Much Are You Carrying?

WOMAN BEHIND THE MASK
Healing Her From The Pains Of Her Past

THE FIGHT OF MY LIFE
Is There Anything Too Hard For The Lord?

WOMAN TO WOMAN, A COLLECTION OF POETRY
Speaking To Women About Life, Purpose & Destiny

MAN TO MAN, A COLLECTION OF POETRY
Speaking To Men About Life, Purpose & Destiny

About the Author

Prophetess Elizabeth Perkins is the Founder of Power In The Word Fellowship and Elizabeth Perkins Ministries. She walks in a Prophetic, Apostolic and Evangelistic Anointing. She has preached the Gospel in the U.S. and Internationally. She has traveled to Africa where she preached and held conferences in Nigeria. In Nigeria, she preached the Word of God in Benin City, Wari, Sapele in Delta State and other villages.

She has worked in a number of areas in her professional career. She has served as a Teacher in the Houston Independent School District and CEP Charter School. She labored in runaway homes for girls and transitional living centers for youth in Tulsa, Oklahoma. In her journey of education and teaching at risk girls, she understood one of her assignments was to help girls change their world. As a result of her passion for helping girls from all walks of life, she recently launched Elizabeth University, an Educational Training School for Girls where she provides classes and seminars.

She is a Poet, Trailblazer and Creator of Elizabeth Publishing House where she houses her books and poetry collections. She is the author of Excess Baggage, Excess Baggage Workbook, Woman Behind The Mask, The Fight Of My Life, Woman To Woman Collection of Poetry and Man To Man Collection of Poetry which are two Powerful Poetry Books. She is also the founder of Excess Baggage Conference, Woman Behind The Mask Conference which was birthed and designed to heal women from their pains of their past and The Fight Of My Life Conference.

Prophetess Elizabeth Perkins has been a native of Houston since 1987. She served 8 years in the United States Naval Reserves where she received an Honorable Discharge. She received her Bachelors of Arts in Political Science and English from Prairie View A&M University and her Master's Degree in Theology from Oral Roberts University School of Theology and Missions in Tulsa, Oklahoma.

As an Intercessor and a Prayer Warrior, Prophetess Elizabeth Perkins messages of truth, encouragement and deliverance have touched the lives of people who have struggled with the pains from their past, such as abandonment, depression, low self-esteem, suicide, abortion and other inward scars.

She currently host ministry revivals, seminars, workshops and conferences. She continues to write books and educational training manuals. As a Prophetess and a Pastor in the Kingdom of God, she is a woman who is submitted to the will of the Lord.

Prophetess Elizabeth Perkins Ministries is manifest with compassion for the lost, troubled souls and the forgotten as well as healing, deliverance and miracles. She is fully persuaded her ministry is to set the captives free and release them into their destiny.

To Contact

Prophetess Elizabeth Perkins

In The U.S. Write:

Elizabeth Perkins Ministries
P.O. Box 271152
Houston, TX 77277

PowerInTheWordFellowship.org
elizabethperkinsma@yahoo.com

www.ingramcontent.com/pod-product-compliance
Lightning Source LLC
Chambersburg PA
CBHW060111170426
43198CB00010B/856